Human Service Organizations
and Their Publications:
A Directory of Selected Sources

Edited by

Francine M. DeFranco and Donna L. Ferullo

Table of Contents

FOREWORD

During the 1991 midwinter meeting of the Association of College and Research Libraries, Education Behavioral Sciences Section, Social Work/Social Welfare Committee, a suggestion was made that the committee produce a directory that would bring together in one source the human service organizations that compile and publish information. Frequently, these organizations are the sole providers of the qualitative and quantitative information in which they specialize. The materials that these organizations provide, however, are often difficult to locate in traditional reference sources. Therefore, members of the ACRL felt that human service researchers, advocates, lobbyists, educators, and managers would benefit greatly from a directory of this kind.

Scope

The directory provides contact information and a list of publications for selected human service organizations throughout the United States. The original list of organizations, associations, institutes, and foundations chosen for inclusion were culled from the personal lists of committee members and from such sources as the *Encyclopedia of Associations* and the *Foundation Directory*. Subsequently, additional organizations were added based on the recommendations of committee members whose knowledge, skills, and experience serve researchers and faculty in academic institutions throughout the United States. Due to the prolific publications of major association presses such as the American Psychological Association, and large government agencies such as the Department of Health and Human Services, the materials produced by these organizations was not included.

To be listed in the directory, an organization, institution, agency, or foundation must be involved in the work of research, social service, advocacy, or lobbying and must provide statistical or descriptive information relating to the social issue(s) or oppressed group(s) that they represent. The entries represent a variety of mostly nonprofit organizations—some well-known, some lesser known—whose publications are not usually available through mainstream press sources. The titles listed in each entry represent the scope and depth of the publications produced by that organization. This directory is intended to provide both the titles of recently published, hard-to-find human service resources, and the contact information necessary to access these products.

Methodology

Initially, the committee members were assigned specific organizations to review for possible inclusion. Additional entries were selected by committee members from within the scope of broad subject areas such as, but not limited to, child welfare, health, violence, social policy, and oppressed groups. At several points, organizations were reviewed and those that could not be contacted via letter or phone, or those deemed beyond the scope of the guidelines, were deleted from the list. Each entry includes the following information:

- Entry number
- Name
- Address
- Phone and/or toll-free number, if available
- Fax number, if available
- Internet site, if available
- Brief description of agency, including history and goals
- Titles of publications
- Subject headings

Entries are arranged in alphabetical order by organization name. The publication titles included with each entry represent a selective list of sources representing the scope of the organization. Using the Library of Congress subject headings as a guide, each entry has been assigned a maximum of three subject headings. These subject headings—which are helpful in locating information on a particular topic, population, or social concern—will expand the user's access to information beyond what is listed in the directory.

Following the entries are indexes by title, subject, and state.

Users should locate information within the directory by consulting the index that best corresponds to their particular research need. For example, to find organizations or information sources concerned with the homeless, check the Subject Index under the term "homelessness." If you know the title of a source, such as *Nation's Health,* and wish to locate the organization that publishes it, check the Title Index. To locate the names and addresses of social services organizations within a particular region, check the State Index.

Contributors

Contributors to the directory were committee members from the Social Work/Social Welfare Committee, 1991–1994. Francine M. DeFranco served as Chair of the committee and Donna L. Ferullo served as Project Coordinator. Donna Ferullo was responsible for the entry format as well as inputting the information from the contributors and assigning the subject headings. Francine DeFranco wrote the introduction to the directory and, along with Donna Ferullo, reviewed the entries. To the best of our knowledge, at the time of submission, all of the information contained in the directory is accurate. Questions or suggestions regarding entries can be addressed to either of the committee members named above. A list of the contributors and their academic affiliations follows the introduction.

Acknowledgments

We would like to thank Jane Johnson whose initiative and energy led to the commencement of this project. It was her contagious enthusiasm that helped us to continue this project when she was unable to do so. Special thanks are also extended to Jennifer Keuhn and Judith Segal, former members of the Social Work/Social Welfare Committee, for contributing their personal lists of organizations. This information provided the framework to begin this project. We would also like thank Gary McMillan, Howard University, for his recommendations of additional organizations as suitable candidates for inclusion in this work.

We would like to express our gratitude to the Association of College and Research Libraries, Education and Behavioral Sciences Section, Social Work/Social Welfare Committee members, 1991–1995, whose interest, contributions and hard work made this project a reality. We are especially grateful to Philip Visconti of Boston College, Social Work Library for his assistance in contacting each of the organizations for information, brochures and publication catalogs. The members of the Social Work/Social Welfare Committee would like to thank the Association of College and Research Libraries, Education and Behavioral Sciences Section, Publication Committee for their thoughtful comments on an earlier draft of this manuscript.

Francine M. DeFranco
University of Connecticut
February 1996

LIST OF CONTRIBUTORS

Mark Berg, Reference Librarian
Social Work Library, Boston College

Corryn Crosby-Muilenburg, Social Science Bibliographer
Humboldt State University

Francine M. DeFranco, Head of Reference
Harleigh B. Trecker Library, University of Connecticut

Donna Ferullo, Head Librarian
Social Work Library, Boston College

Ellen D. Gilbert, Social Science Librarian
Alexander Library, Rutgers University

Martin Jamison, Head
Social Work Library, Ohio State University

Rebecca L. Johnson, Reference Librarian
University of Iowa

Angela S. W. Lee, Head
Social Work Library, University of Washington

Ellie Marsh, Associate Librarian for Public Service
University of North Carolina at Asheville

Darlene P. Nichols, Social Work Librarian
Social Work Library, University of Michigan

Susan Niewenhous, Reference Coordinator and Electronic Resources Librarian
Lewis-Clark State College

Sue Schub, Social Work Librarian
Bobst Library, New York University

Cathy Seitz Whitaker, formerly Social Work Librarian
University of Pittsburgh

[1]
ADVOCATES FOR YOUTH

1025 Vermont Avenue, N.W., Suite 200
Washington, DC 20005
(202) 347-5700
(202) 347-2263 Fax .

History and Goals: This agency works to reduce the incidence of unintended teenage pregnancy, to prevent the spread of HIV among adolescents, and to assure minors' access to family planning information and services. It was established in 1980 and was previously called the Center for Population Options. The agency maintains a library and speaker's bureau and also compiles statistics.

Titles:

Adolescents and Abortion: Choice in Crisis. 1990
Adolescents and Unsafe Abortion in Developing Countries: A Preventable Tragedy. 1992
AIDS and Adolescents. Serial
Clinic News. Quarterly
Guide to Implementing TAP: Teens for Aids Prevention Project. 1990
Linkx. Quarterly
Options. Quarterly
Passages. Quarterly
Teenage Pregnancy and Too-Early Childbearing: Public Costs, Personal Consequences. 1992

Subject Headings:

Adolescence
AIDS disease
Teenage pregnancy

[2]
AL-ANON FAMILY GROUP HEADQUARTERS

P.O. Box 862
Mid-town Station, NY 10018-0862
(212) 302-7240
(800) 356-9996
(718) 260-8276 Fax

History and Goals: The Al-Anon Family Groups are a fellowship of relatives and friends of alcoholics who share their experience, strength and hope in order to solve their common problems. This organization was founded in 1951.

Titles:

Al-Anon Faces Alcoholism. 1992
Al-Anon Family Groups: Formerly Living With An Alcoholic. 1991
Al-Anon's Twelve Concepts of Service, 1990-91. Rev. ed. 1990
Al-Anon's Twelve Steps & Twelve Traditions. 1994
Alateen, A Day at a Time. 1992
Alateen—Hope for Children of Alcoholics. 1992
As We Understood: A Collection of Spiritual Insights. 1995
Courage to Change: One Day at a Time in Al-Anon II. 1992
Digest of Al-Anon & Alateen Policies 1990–91. Rev. ed. 1990
From Survival to Recovery: Growing Up in an Alcoholic Home. 1995

How Al-Anon Works for Families and Friends of Alcoholics. 1995
In All Our Affairs: Making Crisis Work For You. 1990
One Day at a Time in Al-Anon. 1990
When I Got Busy, I Got Better. 1994

Subject Headings:
Alcoholics
Alcoholism
Substance abuse

[3]
ALCOHOLICS ANONYMOUS WORLD SERVICES
P.O. Box 459
Grand Central Station
New York, NY 10163
(212) 870-3312
(212) 870-3137 Fax
Internet Site: http://solar.rtd.utk/~al-anon/index.html

History and Goals: This is the publishing division of Alcoholics Anonymous and it publishes and sells AA literature and audiovisual materials based on the Twelve Step recovery program. AA is a nonprofit organization that is supported by membership contributions and publication sales. The goal of AA is to help its members stay sober and to help others achieve sobriety.

Titles:
The A.A. Service Manual. 1990
Alcoholics Anonymous Comes of Age: A Brief History of A.A. 1990
Alcoholics Anonymous: The Story of How Many Thousands of Men and Women Have Recovered from Alcoholism. 1994
But for the Grace of God . . . How Intergroups and Central Offices Carried the Message of Alcoholism in the 1940s. 1995
Twelve Concepts for World Service. 1991
Twelve Steps and Twelve Traditions. 1993

Subject Headings:
Alcoholics
Alcoholism
Substance abuse

[4]
ALAN GUTTMACHER INSTITUTE
120 Wall Street
New York, NY 10005
(212) 248-1111
(212) 248-1951 Fax
Internet Site: http://www.iti.com/iti/kzpg/agi.html

History and Goals: This nonprofit corporation, founded in 1968, is dedicated to public education, research, and policy analysis on reproductive health issues. The Institute compiles statistics, offers technical assistance, and conducts research.

Titles:

Abortion Factbook, 1992 Edition: Readings, Trends, and State and Local Data to 1988. 1992
Family Planning Perspectives. Bimonthly
Health Care Reform: A Unique Opportunity to Provide Balance and Equity to the Provision of Reproductive Health Services. 1993
International Family Planning Perspectives. Quarterly
The Politics of Blame. 1995
Preventing Pregnancy, Protecting Health: A New Look at Birth Control Choices in the United States. 1991.
Sex and American Teenagers. 1994
State Reproductive Health Monitor: Legislative Proposals and Actions. Quarterly
Teenage Pregnancy in Industrialized Countries. 1986.
Testing Positive: Sexually Transmitted Disease and the Public Health Response. 1993
Today's Adolescents, Tomorrow's Parents: A Portrait of the Americas. 1990
Washington Memo. 20 issues/year
Women at Risk of Unintended Pregnancy, 1990 Estimates: The Need for Family Planning Services, Each State and County. 1993

Subject Headings:
Birth control
Population policy
Teenage pregnancy

[5]
ALEXANDER GRAHAM BELL ASSOCIATION FOR THE DEAF
3417 Volta Place NW
Washington, DC 20007-2778
(202) 337-5220 TDD and Voice

History and Goals: This nonprofit membership organization was organized in 1890 to encourage the use of residual hearing and the teaching of speech and speech-reading. The Association seeks to promote better public understanding of hearing loss in adult and children, to provide training for teachers of the hearing impaired, and to encourage research on auditory/verbal communication.

Titles:

The ADA and the Hearing Impaired Consumer. 1992
Choices in Deafness: A Parent's Guide. 1987
Communication and Adult Hearing Loss. 1993
Communication Skills in Hearing Impaired Children. 1992
Coping With Hearing Loss: A Guide for Adults and Their Families. 1993
Cued Speech Resource Guide for Parents of Deaf Children. 1992
Hearing Aids: Recent Developments. 1993
Let's Converse: A "How To" Guide to Develop and Expand Conversational Skills of Children and Teenagers Who are Hearing Impaired. 1994
Listening to Learn: A Handbook for Parents with Hearing-Impaired Children. 1990
Screening Children for Auditory Function. 1992
Selected Issues in Adolescence and Deafness. 1991

Subject Headings:
Deafness
Hearing disorders

[6]
ALZHEIMER'S ASSOCIATION
919 North Michigan Avenue
Suite 1000
Chicago, IL 60611-1676
(312) 335-8700
(800) 272-3900
(312) 335-1110 Fax
Internet Site: http://www.alz.org/

History and Goals: The Alzheimer's Association was founded in 1980 to promote research on the treatment, cure, and causes of Alzheimer's disease. The Association provides educational programs and works to develop support for relatives of victims of Alzheimer's disease.

Titles:

The 36 Hour Day: A Family Guide to Caring for Persons with Alzheimer's Disease, Related Dementing Illnesses, and Memory Loss Later in Life. 1991
Alzheimer Care Demonstration Evaluation Report. 1991
Alzheimer Care Program Guide. 1991
Alzheimer's Advocates Handbook. 1993
An Annotated Bibliography of Adult Day Programs and Dementia Care. 1992
Directory of Adult Respite Care Funded or Provided by State Governments. 1993
Family Guide for Alzheimer Care in Residential Settings. 1992
A Guide to Survival: The Alzheimer Dilemma. 1992
Guidelines for Dignity: Goals of Specialized Alzheimer/Dementia Care in Residential Settings. 1992
Long Term Care: The Hidden Health Care Crisis in Rural America. 1994
1995 Informational Material. 1995
Public Policy Update. Quarterly
Respite Care Manual. 1989
Taking Care: Alzheimer/Dementia Respite Care Experiences and Advice. 1992
The Vanishing Mind. 1991

Subject Headings:
Alzheimer's disease
Dementia

[7]
AMERICAN ASSOCIATION FOR COUNSELING AND DEVELOPMENT
5999 Stevenson Avenue
Alexandria, VA 22304-3300
(703) 823-9800
(800) 347-6647
(703) 823-0252 Fax

History and Goals: The AACD was founded in 1952 by counseling professionals to promote the advancement of counseling in education, government, industry, and private practice. The Association conducts research, provides training, publishes extensively, and serves as an advocate for the profession.

Titles:
Assessment and Knowledge of Gerontological Counselor Knowledge and Skills. 1990
Career Development. Quarterly
Challenges of Cultural and Racial Diversity to Counseling. 1991
Counseling Victims of Violence. 1991
Counselor Preparation. 7th ed. 1990-1992
Journal for Specialists in Group Work. Quarterly
Journal of Counseling and Development. Bimonthly
Journal of Multicultural Counseling and Development. Quarterly
Rehabilitation Counseling Bulletin. Quarterly

Subject Headings:
Counseling
Vocational guidance

[8]
AMERICAN ASSOCIATION FOR MARRIAGE AND FAMILY THERAPY
1133 15th St. NW, Suite 300
Washington, DC 20005-2710
(202) 452-0109
(202) 223-2329 Fax

History and Goals: The AAMFT was founded in 1942 by marriage and family therapists and related professionals to advance the discipline of marriage and family therapy as a means of creating family and marital well-being. AAMFT seeks to establish standards in the field, provide training and referral, facilitate research, and represent the discipline to the government and the public.

Titles:
AAMFT Code of Ethical Principles for Marriage and Family Therapists. 1985
The AAMFT, Fifty Years of Marital and Family Therapy. 1992
American Association for Marriage and Family Therapy Ethics Casebook. 1994
Employment and Training: Strategies to Reduce Family Poverty. 1993
Family Therapy Glossary. Rev. ed. 1992
Family Therapy News. Bimonthly
Journal of Marital and Family Therapy. Quarterly
Marriage and Family Therapy: Regulating the Profession. 1993
Register of Marriage and Family Therapy Providers. Serial

Subject Headings:
Family therapy
Marriage counseling

[9]
AMERICAN ASSOCIATION OF CHILDREN'S RESIDENTIAL CENTERS
1021 Prince Street
Alexandria, VA 22314-2971
(703) 838-7522
(703) 684-5968 Fax

History and Goals: The AARC is committed to ensure the highest standard of care for the treatment of the emotionally disturbed children and adolescents and for increasing the support and interests for both the children and their families. Founded in 1956, the Association provides a national, interdisciplinary exchange of research and development and serves as a source of current information in this area.

Titles:
Contribution to Residential Treatment Annual
Directory of Organizational Members. Annual
Residential Treatment for Children and Youth. Quarterly
Residential Treatment News. Bimonthly

Subject Headings:
Children
Residential treatment
Youth

[10]
AMERICAN ASSOCIATION OF RETIRED PERSONS
601 E Street, NW
Washington, DC 20049
(202) 434-2277
(202) 434-2330 Fax

History and Goals: Founded in 1958, the AARP, with a current membership of more than 32 million, has become a very viable and vocal advocate for the needs and rights of older people. Major concerns of the AARP include health care, minority affairs, women's rights and equity for older employees.

Titles:
AARP News Bulletin. Monthly
Assisted Living in the United States. 1993
Connecting the Generations: A Guide to Intergenerational Resources. 1994
Health Care Reform in America: Where the Public Stands. 1993
Life Changes and Their Effects on Public Benefits. 1991
Modern Maturity. Bimonthly
Old and Alone in Rural America. 1993
Organizing Your Future: A Guide to Decision Making in Your Later Years. 1991
A Practical Guide to Nursing Home Advocacy. 1991
Progress in Elderly Housing: Who's Left Behind. 1993
A Study of Older Hispanics. 1994
Towards a Just and Caring Society: AARP Public Policy Agenda. Annual
Who Decides If You Can't? 1994
Women, Pensions and Divorce. 1993

Subject Headings:
Aged

[11]
AMERICAN ASSOCIATION OF STATE SOCIAL WORK BOARDS
400 South Ridge Parkway, Suite B
Culpeper, VA 22701
(703) 829-6880
(703) 829-0142 Fax

History and Goals: The AASSWB, founded in 1979, establishes national regulatory standards for the practice of social work. The Association provides uniform examinations to state boards, facilitates the exchange of information concerning the regulation of social workers, promotes research on legal regulations for social work, and strives to educate the public regarding good social work practice.

Titles:

AASSWB Newsletter. Quarterly

American Association of State Social Work Boards Study Guide. 1993

Reciprocity and Endorsement Summary. 1991

Social Work Laws and Board Regulations: A State Comparison Summary. 1995

State Comparison of Social Work Laws and Regulations. Annual

Subject Headings:

Social case work

Social service

[12]

AMERICAN ASSOCIATION ON MENTAL RETARDATION

444 North Capitol Street, NW, Suite 846

Washington, DC 20001-1512

(202) 387-1968

(800) 424-3688

History and Goals: The AAMR was founded in 1876. This is an interdisciplinary association that helps review and reshape public policy and encourage research and education regarding mental retardation issues. The AAMR promotes quality services for those with mental retardation and their families.

Titles:

American Journal on Mental Retardation. Bimonthly

Emerging Issues in Family Support. 1992

Foster Family Care for Persons With Mental Retardation. 1992

How to Teach Self-Instruction of Job Skills. 1994

Life Course Perspectives on Adulthood and Old Age. 1994

Mental Retardation: Definition, Classification, and Systems of Support. 9th ed. 1992

The Milwaukee Project: Preventing Mental Retardation in Children at Risk. 1988

News & Notes. Quarterly

Recognizing Community Choices by Individuals with Profound Disabilities: An Assessment. 1994

Residential Services and Developmental Disabilities in the United States. 1992

The Self Advocacy Movement by People with Developmental Disabilities: A Demographic Study and Directory of Self-Advocacy Groups in the United States. 1994

Subject Headings:

Developmentally disabled

Handicapped

Mental retardation

[13]

AMERICAN CORRECTIONAL ASSOCIATION

8025 Laurel Lakes Ct.
Laurel, MD 20707-5075
(301) 206-5100
(800) 222-5646
(301) 302-5061 Fax

History and Goals: Founded in 1870, the American Correctional Association strives to improve correctional standards, including selection of personnel, care, supervision, education, training, employment, treatment, and post-release adjustment of inmates. They also provide information for non-association publications.

Titles:

Addiction Letter. Monthly
AIDS Education and Prevention: An Interdisciplinary Journal. Quarterly
Considering Marriage: A Premarital Workbook for Couples Separated by Incarceration. 1994
Correctional and Juvenile Justice Training Directory. 2nd ed. 1991
Directory of Juvenile and Adult Correctional Departments, Institutions, Agencies, and Paroling Authorities. 1995
Drug, Alcohol, and Other Addictions: A Directory of Treatment Centers and Prevention Programs Nationwide. 2nd ed. 1993
The Gang Journal: An Interdisciplinary Research Quarterly. Quarterly
International Journal of Offender Therapy. Quarterly
Legal Issues for Correctional Staff. 1994
National Jail and Adult Detention Directory. 1990
Prison Violence in America. 2nd ed. 1994
Probation and Parole Directory. 1992
Short-Term Group Counseling. 1993
Standards for Adult Community Residential Services. 1995
State of Corrections—Proceedings 1993. Annual
Vital Statistics in Corrections. 1994

Subject Headings:

Corrections
Criminal psychology
Prisoners

[14]

AMERICAN COUNCIL ON ALCOHOLISM

2522 St. Paul St.
Baltimore, MD 21218
(410) 889-0100
(800) 527-5344
(410) 889-0100 Fax

History and Goals: Formed as a regional association in 1953, the Council was incorporated as a national organization in 1976. ACA advances the concept, at the national and state levels, that alcoholism is an identifiable, treatable illness. ACA advances the illness concept through its government relations and professional and educational outreach.

Titles:
ACA Journal. Quarterly
ACA News. Monthly
Controversies in the Addiction Field. 1994
Directions of Alcoholism Councils in America. Serial
Legal Alcohol vs. Illegal Drugs: Making the Distinction. 1988
Network: An Educational/Healthy Lifestyle Network. Quarterly

Subject Headings:
Alcohol
Alcoholism
Substance abuse

[15]
AMERICAN ENTERPRISE INSTITUTE FOR PUBLIC POLICY RESEARCH
1150 17th Street NW
Washington, DC 20036
(202) 862-5800
(202) 862-7178 Fax

History and Goals: The Institute seeks to promote open and competitive enterprise and limited government. Since 1943, the AEI has done research in foreign policy, national defense, domestic and international economic policy and social and political issues.

Titles:
The American Enterprise. Monthly
Character and Cops: Ethics in Policing. 1994
Competition and Monopoly in Medical Care. 1994
Cost Shifting in Health Care: Separating Evidence from Rhetoric. 1994
Economic Effects of Health Care Reform. 1994
Financial Markets and Public Policy in the Year 2000. 1994
Health Care Choices: Using Private Contracts for Health Reform. 1994
New Issues in Depressive Illness. 1993
On the Other Hand . . . Reflections on Economics, Economists, and Politics. 1995
Presidential Economics: The Making of Economic Policy from Roosevelt to Clinton. 3rd rev. ed.
   1994
Referendums Around the World. 1994
Tyranny of Numbers: Mismeasurement and Misrule. 1995

Subject Headings:
Economic policy
Public policy

[16]
AMERICAN FOUNDATION FOR THE BLIND
11 Penn Plaza, Suite 300
New York, NY 10001
(212) 502-7600
(800) AFB-LIND
(212) 502-7777 Fax

History and Goals: The AFB works for equality of opportunity and access for blind people. The foundation serves as an advisor and advocate on public policy, provides products and services, and makes information and education programs available.

Titles:

The Burns Braille Transcription Dictionary. 1992

The Development of Social Skills by Blind and Visually Impaired Students: Exploratory Studies and Strategies. 1992

Directory of Camps for Blind and Visually Impaired Children, Youth and Adults. 1989

Directory of Services for Blind and Visually Impaired Persons in the United States. 24th ed. 1993

Early Focus: Working with Young Blind and Visually Impaired Children and Their Families. 1992

Foundations of Braille Literacy. 1994

Independence Without Sight and Sound: Suggestions for Practitioners Working with Deaf-Blind Adults. 1993

Journal of Visual Impairment and Blindness. 10/year

Mainstreaming and the American Dream: Sociological Perspectives on Parental Coping with Blind and Visually Impaired Children. 1992

A Picture is Worth a Thousand Words for Blind and Visually Impaired Persons Too! An Introduction to Audio Description. 1991

Sources of Products for Blind and Visually Impaired Persons. 1991

Tactile Graphics. 1992

Vision and Aging: Crossroads for Service Delivery. 1992

Visual Impairment: An Overview. 1990

Subject Headings:

Blind

Vision disorders

Visually handicapped

[17]
AMERICAN GERIATRICS SOCIETY

770 Lexington Avenue, Suite 300
New York, NY 10021
(212) 308-1414
(800) 247-4779
(212) 832-8646 Fax

History and Goals: The AGS, founded in 1942, seeks to improve the health and well-being of older adults through promoting the practice of geriatrics, promoting research which addresses the health care of older people, and lobbying for public policies which will focus on the improvement of health care for older people.

Titles:

AGS Newsletter. Bimonthly

American Geriatrics Society Complete Guide to Aging and Health. 1995

Introduction to Methodologies for Clinical Research in Geriatrics. 1993

Journal of the American Geriatrics Society. Monthly

Medical Treatment Decisions Concerning Elderly Persons. 1991

New Issues in Depressive Illness. 1993

Psychotherapeutic Medications in the Nursing Home. 1992

Use of Drugs of Questionable Efficacy in the Elderly. 1991

Voluntary Active Euthanasia. 1990

Subject Headings:
Aged
Aging
Gerontology

[18]
AMERICAN HOSPITAL ASSOCIATION
1 North Franklin
Chicago, IL 60606
(312) 422-3000
(800) AHA-2626 (Order Department only)
(312) 422-2796 Fax

History and Goals: Founded in 1898, the AHA serves health care institutions, individuals and the public. It compiles statistics, conducts research, and provides education in the health care field.

Titles:
Acronyms and Initialisms in Health Care Administration. 1986
AHA Directory of Health Care Professionals. Annual
AHA Guide to the Health Care Field. Annual
AHA Hospital Statistics. Annual
AHA News. Weekly
Customizing an Orientation Program for New Social Workers. 1992
Essentials for Directors of Social Work Programs in Health Care. 1990
Hospital Literature Index. Quarterly
Hospitals. Biweekly
Managing Cultural Diversity in the Work Place. 1992
Social Work in Health Care: A Review of the Literature. 1988
Strategic Responses to a Capitating Marketplace. 1995
Working from Within: Integrating Rural Health Care. 1993

Subject Headings:
Health services administration
Hospitals
Medical social work

[19]
AMERICAN HUMANE ASSOCIATION
63 Inverness Drive East
Englewood, CO 80112-5117
(303) 792-9900
(303) 792-5333 Fax

History and Goals: Founded in 1877, the AHA has two divisions. The Animal Protection Division is dedicated to the protection of animals. The American Association for Protecting Children works to improve services for children and families. The AAPC division offers in service training, provides expert assistance, conducts research on child abuse, and advocates legislation on the national and state level to protect children.

Titles:

Annotated Bibliography of Resources on Cultural Competence and Cultural Diversity in Child Welfare/Child Protection Services. 1993

Call to Competence: Child Protective Services Training and Evaluation. 1995

Child Welfare Workload Analysis and Resource Management: WARM Workshop and Practitioner's Meeting—Resource Manual. 1993

First Annual Roundtable on Outcome Measures in Child Welfare Services: Summary of the Proceedings. 1993

Guidelines for Schools. 1991

Helping in Child Protective Services: A Casebook Handbook. Rev. ed. 1992

Highlight of Official Child Neglect and Abuse Reporting. 1987

Protecting Children. Quarterly

Risk Assessment Revisited. 1994

Selected Annotated Readings on Outcome Measures in Child Welfare. 1993

Training Guide for Recognizing and Reporting Child Abuse. 1995

Subject Headings:

Child abuse

Child welfare

Children

[20]
AMERICAN PUBLIC HEALTH ASSOCIATION

1015 15th Street NW
Washington, DC 20005-3300
(202) 789-5600
(202) 789-5681 Fax

History and Goals: Founded in 1872, APHA is an organization for public health professionals. Its primary goal is to set standards, develop policies, participate in research, and disseminate information on all matters concerning public health.

Titles:

American Journal of Public Health. Monthly

Caring for Our Children. 1992

A Century of Caring: A Celebration of Public Health Nursing in the United States 1893–1993. 1993

Control of Communicable Diseases Manual. 1995

Nation's Health. Monthly

Subject Headings:

Medical care

Public health

[21]
AMERICAN PUBLIC WELFARE ASSOCIATION

810 First Street NE Suite 500
Washington, DC 20002-4267
(202) 682-0100
(202) 289-6555 Fax

History and Goals: The American Public Welfare Association was founded in 1930 to serve public welfare agencies, their staff, and those interested in public welfare. The Association publishes and conducts research.

Titles:

Characteristics of Children in Substitute and Adoptive Care. 1993

Elder Abuse in the United States: An Issue Paper. 1990

Fact Book on Public Child Welfare Services and Staff. 1991

Guidelines for a Model System of Protective Services for Abused and Neglected Children and Their Families. 1988

Public Welfare Directory. Annual

Public Welfare Journal. Quarterly

Responsibility, Work, Pride: The Values of Welfare Reform. 1994

This Week in Washington. Weekly

Subject Headings:

Public welfare

[22]

THE ARC

500 E. Border Street

Suite 300

Arlington, TX 76010

(817) 261-6003

(817) 227-3491 Fax

Internet Site: http://fohnix.metronet.com/~thearc/welcome.html

History and Goals: This Association, formerly called the Association for Retarded Citizens of the United States, was founded in 1950 to serve those interested in mental retardation. ARC works on all levels of government to promote research, services, and legislation which will serve the mentally retarded and their families.

Titles:

Advocates' Voice. Triannual

ARC Government Report. Semimonthly

The ARC Now. Monthly

The ARC Today. Bimonthly

Directory of Self-Advocacy Programs. 1993

Making a Difference: Career Opportunities in Disability-Related Fields. 1993

Position Statements of the ARC. 1992

Subject Headings:

Mental retardation

[23]

ASSOCIATION FOR THE CARE OF CHILDREN'S HEALTH

7910 Woodmont Avenue, Suite 300

Bethesda, MD 20814

(301) 654-6549

(301) 986-4553 Fax

History and Goals: Founded in 1965, the Association is a nonprofit educational and advocacy organization. Its primary focus is to ensure that all aspects of children's health are family-centered, psychosocially sound and developmentally supportive. ACCH membership represents health and social services professionals, educators, researchers, parents, and community leaders.

Titles:
The ACCH Advocate. Semiannual
ACCH Network. Quarterly
ACCH News. Bimonthly
Children's Health Care. Quarterly

Subject Headings:
Child health services
Children
Social work with children

[24]
BLACK GAY AND LESBIAN LEADERSHIP FORUM
1219 South La Brea Avenue
Los Angeles, CA 90019
(213) 964-7820
(213) 964-7830 Fax

History and Goals: Founded in 1988, the Black Gay and Lesbian Leadership Forum was established as an alternative for African American lesbians and gay men to address issues facing their community and to exchange information. It sponsors the annual National Black Gay and Lesbian Conference. It has formed the AIDS Prevention Team, one of the first organizations to address all aspects of services to the African American HIV-infected community.

Titles:
AIDS Prevention Team Treatment Update and Information. Monthly

Subject Headings:
Gays
Homosexuality
Lesbians

[25]
BREAD FOR THE WORLD INSTITUTE
1100 Wayne Avenue, Suite 1000
Silver Spring, MD 20910
(301) 608-2400
(301) 608-2401 Fax

History and Goals: Bread for the World Institute strives to provide information to citizens on the condition of world hunger for the purpose of promoting activities to influence the politics and policies to deal with this concern. Maintained by Bread for the World, the Institute (the research/education arm) focuses on issues related to hunger such as employment, third world debt, financial assistance to needy countries, defense spending, and farming. Additionally, the Institute sponsors research and activities, such as workshops and seminars, as a means of educating those interested in the causes and effects of world hunger.

Titles:
Background Papers. 10/year
Bread for the World Newsletter. 8/year
Hunger Report. Annual (since 1990)
Peace, Development, and People of the Horn of Africa. 1992

Subject Headings:
Hunger

[26]
BROOKINGS INSTITUTION
1775 Massachusetts Ave., NW
Washington, DC 20036
(202) 797-6000
(202) 797-6004 Fax
Internet Site: gopher://brook/edu:70/1

History and Goals: Founded in 1916, Brookings is an independent organization devoted to nonpartisan research, education, and publication in the fields of economics, government, and foreign policy. Brookings divisions include the Center for Public Policy Education; Economic Studies; External Affairs, Foreign Policy Studies; Government Studies; Public Affairs; and a Social Science Computations Center. Each division conducts numerous conferences, forums, and seminars.

Titles:
Brookings Newsletter. Quarterly
Brookings Papers on Economic Activity. Semiannual
Brookings Review. Quarterly
Directory of Scholars. Annual
How Russia Became a Market Economy. 1995
Reinventing Government: Appraising the National Performance Review. 1994
Verdict: Assessing the Civil Jury System. 1993

Subject Headings:
Education
Public policy
Research

[27]
CENTER FOR FOREIGN POLICY DEVELOPMENT
Brown University
Box 1948
Providence, RI 02912
(401) 863-3465
(401) 863-7440 Fax

History and Goals: The Center was established in 1981 and conducts research on U.S. national security policy, nuclear weapons issues, immigration, and world economics. The Center also provides reproducible curricular units.

Titles:
The Arab-Israeli Conflict: Looking for a Lasting Peace. 1992
Coming to Terms With Power: U.S. Choices After World War II. 1992
Facing a Disintegrated Soviet Union. 1992

Global Environmental Problems: Implications for U.S. Policy. 1992
In the Shadow of the Cold War: The Caribbean and Central America in U.S. Foreign Policy. 1993
The Role of the United States in a Changing World. 1992
U.S. Immigration Policy in an Unsettled World. 1992
U.S. Trade Policy: Competing in a Global Economy. 1993

Subject Headings:
Economics
Immigrants
International relations

[28]
CENTER FOR LAW AND SOCIAL POLICY
1616 P Street NW, Suite 150
Washington, DC 20036
(202) 328-5140
(202) 328-5195 Fax
Internet Site: http://epn.org/clasp.html

History and Goals: CLASP was founded in 1969. The Center is a public-interest law organization involved with legal advocacy for the poor and underrepresented.

Titles:
Adolescent Mothers, AFDC and JOBS. 1994
Family Matters. Quarterly
Finding Funding for JOBS. 1992
The JOBS Program: Answers and Questions. 2nd ed. 1992
Public Benefit Issues in Divorce Cases: A Manual for Lawyers and Paralegals. 1994
The Rush to "Reform": 1992 State AFDC Legislative and Waiver Actions. 1992
Selected Background Material on Welfare Programs. 1992
States Update. 10/year
The Temporary Family Assistance Block Grant. 1995
Turning Promises Into Realities: A Guide to Implementing the Child Support Provisions of the Family Support Act of 1988. 2nd ed. 1991
Welfare Reform on a Budget: What's Happening in JOBS. 1992

Subject Headings:
Children
Family
Public welfare

[29]
CENTER FOR MIGRATION STUDIES
209 Flagg Place
Staten Island, NY 10304-1199
(718) 351-8800

History and Goals: The Center was founded in 1964 and encourages the sociological, demographic, economic and historical study of the world's populations and their movements.

Titles:
CMS Newsletter. Semiannual
The Columbus People: Perspectives in Italian Immigration to the Americas and Australia. 1994

The Demographics of Immigration: A Socio-Demographic Profile of Foreign-Born Population in New York. 1992

In Defense of the Alien: Proceedings of the 1993 CMS National Legal Conference on Immigration and Refugee Policy. 1993

The Immigration Experience in the United States: Policy Implications. 1994

Implementation of the Immigration Act of 1990. 1994

International Migration Review. Quarterly

Legal Immigration Reform in the U.S. 1992

Migration Return: A Bibliographical Overview. 1994

Migrational World Magazine. Bimonthly

The New Second Generation. 1995

The Politics of Migration Policies. 2nd ed. 1993

Population Displacement and Resettlement. 1994

When Borders Don't Divide. 1988

Working with Refugees. 1987

Subject Headings:

Emigration and immigration

Immigrants

[30]
CENTER FOR THE STUDY OF AGING

706 Madison Avenue

Albany, NY 12208

(518) 465-6927

(518) 462-1339 Fax

History and Goals: The Center has provided leadership in the field of health and fitness for older people since 1957. The Center's services include consulting in program planning.

Titles:

Classics in Aging. Series

Physical Activity, Aging, and Sports. Serial

Toward Healthy Aging—International Perspectives. 1994

Subject Headings:

Aged

Aging

Frail elderly

[31]
CENTER FOR THE STUDY OF SOCIAL POLICY

1250 Eye Street, NW Suite 503

Washington, DC 20005-3922

(202) 371-1565

(202) 371-1472 Fax

History and Goals: The Center was founded in 1979 to assist federal, state, and local governments in improving human services for low-income and other disadvantaged populations. Its mission is to effect change through the analysis of existing policies and the development of new ones. It prepares publications in the areas of income maintenance, social services, health care, disability, long-term care, and services to children, youth, and families.

Titles:
The Case for Comprehensive Unemployment Insurance Reform. 1987
Completing the Long-Term Care Continuum: An Income Supplement Strategy. 1988
The "Flip-Side" of Black Families Headed by Women: The Economic Status of Black Men. 1986
Images of the Disabled, Disabling Images. 1987
Making Strategic Use of the Family Preservation and Support Services Program. 1994
Restructuring Medicaid: An Agenda for Change. 2 vol. 1984

Subject Headings:
Children
Family
Social policy

[32]
CENTER FOR WOMEN POLICY STUDIES
2000 P Street, NW
Washington, DC 20036
(202) 872-1770
(202) 296-8962 Fax

History and Goals: The Center for Women Policy Studies, founded in 1972, is an independent institution dedicated to researching policy and advocacy issues relating to the status, needs, and race and gender bias of women. Programs sponsored by the Center incorporate research, advocacy, policy, and education to address the issues of equity, empowerment, health, and economics that concern women today.

Titles:
Earnings Sharing in Social Security: A Model for Reform. 1988
Guide to Resources on Women and AIDS. 2nd ed. 1992
Unjust Punishments: Mandatory HIV Testing of Women Sex Workers and Pregnant Women. 1992
Violence Against Women as Bias Motivated Hate Crime: Defining the Issues. 1991
Women Faculty in the Classroom. 1993
Women of Color in Science, Mathematics and Engineering: A Review of the Literature. 1991
Women, Pregnancy and Substance Abuse. 1991
Women, Welfare and Higher Education: A Selected Annotated Bibliography. 1991

Subject Headings:
Women

[33]
CENTER ON BUDGET AND POLICY PRIORITIES
777 North Capitol Street, N.E.
Suite 705
Washington, DC 20002
(202) 408-1080
(202) 408-1056 Fax
Internet Site: http://epn.org/cbpp.html

History and Goals: Since 1981 the Center has promoted public understanding of the impact of governmental spending policies and programs, and has conducted studies on minorities and poverty.

Titles:

A Hand Up: How State Earned Income Credits Help Working Families Escape Poverty. 1992
Holes in the Safety Net: Poverty Programs and Policies in the States. 1988
Life Under the Spending Caps: The Clinton Fiscal Year 1995 Budget. 1994
Limited Access: Health Care for the Rural Poor. 1991
National General Assistance Survey. 1992
The Personal Responsibility Act. 1994
A Place to Call Home: The Crisis in Housing for the Poor. 1992
Poverty in Rural America: A National Overview. 1989
Where Have All the Dollars Gone? A State-by State Analysis of Income Disparities Over the 1980s.
    1992
White Poverty in America. 1992
WIC Newsletter. 9/year

Subject Headings:

Minorities
Poverty
Social policy

[34]
CENTER ON SOCIAL WELFARE POLICY & LAW

275 7th Avenue, 6th Fl.
New York, NY 10001-6708
(212) 633-6967
(212) 633-6371 Fax

History and Goals: This organization was founded in 1965. It studies significant cases in welfare law, provides information on welfare issues, and develops materials for legal services attorneys and for welfare recipient groups. The CSWPL also maintains a poverty law library.

Titles:

AFDC Program Rules for Advocates: An Overview. 1991
*Finding the Facts: Sources of Statistical Information about the Poverty Population and Those
    Receiving AFDC.* 1992
*Jobless, Penniless, Often Homeless: State General Assistance Cuts Leave "Employables" Struggling for
    Survival.* 1994
Left to the Tender Mercies of the States: The Fate of Poor Families. 1995
Living at the Bottom: An Analysis of AFDC Benefit Levels. 1993
Out of the Arms of Mothers. 1995
Welfare Cutback Litigation, 1991–1994. 1994

Subject Headings:

Child welfare
Poor
Public welfare

[35]

CHILD WELFARE LEAGUE OF AMERICA
440 First St. NW Suite 310
Washington, DC 20001-2085
(202) 638-2952
(202) 638-4004 Fax

History and Goals: Founded in 1920, CWLA focuses on the needs and care of abused, dependent, or neglected children and youth and their families.

Titles:
Adoption Resource Guide: A National Directory of Licensed Agencies. 1991
Child Welfare. Monthly
Child Welfare: A Source Book of Knowledge and Practice. 1984
The Child Welfare State Book. Serial
Children Can't Wait: Reducing Delays in Out-Of-Home Care. 1993
Church Agencies Caring for Children and Families in Crisis. 1994
CWLA 1993 Legislative Agenda: Budget Updates and Issues Brief for the . . . Congress. Annual
CWLA Salary Study. Annual
CWLA Standards. Serial
Developmental Network Approach to Therapeutic Foster Care. 1993
Kinship Care: A Natural Bridge. 1994
Homeworks. Serial

Subject Headings:
Child welfare
Family
Social work with children

[36]

CHILDREN'S DEFENSE FUND
Publications Department
25 E Street, NW
Washington, DC 20001
(202) 662-3652
(202) 662-3530 Fax

History and Goals: CDF is a nonprofit organization that advocates for a strong and effective voice for the children of America, who cannot vote, lobby, or speak out for themselves. CDF pays particular attention to the needs of poor, minority, and disabled children. CDF's goal is to educate the nation about the needs of children and encourage preventive investment in children before they get sick, drop out of school, suffer family breakdown, or get into trouble.

Titles:
Adolescent and Young Adult Fact Book. 1991
A Black Community Crusade and Covenant for Protecting Children. 1995
Building a National Immunization System. 1994
CDF Reports. Monthly
CDF's Child, Youth, and Family Futures Clearinghouse. Bimonthly
Children in the States. 1995
Decade of Indifference: Maternal and Child Health Trends, 1980–1990. 1993

Enforcing Child Support: Are the States Doing the Job? 1994
Health of America's Children. Annual
Health of America's Southern Children: Maternal and Child Health Data Book. 1990
Investing in Our Children's Care. 1993
The Nation's Investment in Children: An Analysis of the President's . . . Budget Proposals. Annual
Progress and Peril: Black Children in America. 1993
State of America's Children. Annual
Wasting America's Future: The Children's Defense Fund's Report on Child Poverty. 1994

Subject Headings:
Child welfare
Teenagers
Youth

[37]
COALITION ON HUMAN NEEDS
1000 Wisconsin Avenue NW
Washington, DC 20007
(202) 342-0726
(202) 342-1132 Fax

History and Goals: Founded in 1981, the Coalition on Human Needs (CHN) is an organization of more than 100 groups who are involved in meeting the needs of low-income families through public assistance, housing, education, medical care, and public policy advocacy. The organization keeps member groups and newsletter subscribers up-to-date with current legislative action concerning human needs and welfare. In addition, the CHN has a special interest in monitoring block grant proposals.

Titles:
Block Grant Missing the Target—An Overview of Findings. 1987
Block Grants, Beyond the Rhetoric. 1987
Coalition on Human Needs Insight/Action. Bimonthly
How the Poor Would Remedy Poverty. 1987
Human Needs Legislative Report. Biweekly
Monitoring Welfare Reform Guide. 1991
National Technical Assistance Directory. 1989

Subject Headings:
Human services
Poor
Public welfare

[38]
CO-DEPENDENTS ANONYMOUS
P.O. Box 33577
Phoenix, AZ 85067-3577
(602) 277-7991
(602) 274-6111 Fax

History and Goals: Founded in 1986, Co-Dependents Anonymous provides support and recovery programs for persons who are co-dependents. The program is similar to that of Alcoholics Anonymous.

Titles:
Co-NNECTIONS. Quarterly

Subject Headings:
Codependency
Substance abuse

[39]
COMMITTEE FOR SINGLE ADOPTIVE PARENTS
P.O. Box 15084
Chevy Chase, MD 20825
(202) 966-6367

History and Goals: Founded in 1973, the Committee for Single Adoptive Parents provides information to adoption agencies, single adoptive parents and to those who would like to become an adoptive parent.

Titles:
Handbook for Single Adoptive Parents. 1992

Subject Headings:
Adoption
Single parents

[40]
THE COMMONWEALTH FUND
One East 75th Street
New York, NY 10021
(212) 535-0400

History and Goals: This philanthropic foundation was created in 1918 by Anna M. Harkness with the goal of enhancing the common good. Today, this is accomplished by trying to help Americans to live healthy and productive lives and to aid specific groups in trying to solve serious problems. The Fund has focused on improving health care, advocating for the aged, educating young people, promoting wellness, and improving the health of minorities. The Fund accomplishes these goals by providing grants and fellowships.

Titles:
Aging and Alone: Profiles and Projections. 1988
Americans' Health Care Concerns: A National Survey. 1992
For the Common Good. 1994
Monitoring Medicaid Managed Care. 1995
The Nation's Great Overlooked Resource: The Contributions of Americans 55+. 1992
Pilot Survey of Young African American Males in Four Cities. 1994
Study of Elderly People in Five Countries—United States, Canada, Germany, Britain, and Japan—Key Findings. 1991
Young People at Risk: Is Prevention Possible? 1988

Subject Headings:
Aged
Medical care

[41]
COMMUNITY SERVICE SOCIETY OF NEW YORK
105 East 22nd Street
New York, NY 10010
(212) 614-5314

History and Goals: Formed in 1939 by the merger of two older organizations, the Society works to identify the needs of the poor in New York City and to provide programs to meet their needs. The CSS also acts as an advocate for those in poverty by keeping the state and federal lawmakers aware of their needs.

Titles:
ACES (Advocacy, Counseling and Entitlement Services). Quarterly
Building Blocks: Community-Based Strategies. 1994
Definitions and Realities of Poverty. 1988
Living in Poverty: Coping on the Welfare Grant. 1990
Poverty in New York City, 1991. 1992
Resources: A Directory of New York City Directories. 2nd ed. 1991
We are the Landlords Now: A Report on Community-Based Housing Management. 1993

Subject Headings:
Poverty
Social service

[42]
COMPUTER USE IN SOCIAL SERVICES NETWORK
University of Texas at Arlington
Box 1912
Arlington, TX 76019-0129
(817) 273-3964
(817) 794-5795 Fax

History and Goals: The Computer Use in Social Services Network, founded in 1981, provides a forum for the exchange of information and resources in the use of computers among professionals working in the social services.

Titles:
CUSSN Newsletter. Quarterly

Subject Headings:
Computers
Social service

[43]
CONCERNED UNITED BIRTHPARENTS
2000 Walker Street
Des Moines, IA 50317
(515) 263-9558
(800) 822-2777

History and Goals: Founded in 1976, the Concerned United Birthparents is an organization of birthparents and others who are interested in reforming adoption laws and in guaranteeing that every mother has an opportunity to make an informed decision concerning whether or not to put her child up for adoption. The CUB would like to change laws related to opening up birth records and to make it easier for birthparents to find relatives lost due to adoption.

Titles:

Adoption Searchbook. 3rd ed. 1991
Birth Bond. 1991
Birthmothers. 1993
Choices, Chances, Changes. 1987
Concerned United Birthparents—Communicator. Monthly
Thoughts for Birthparents Newly Considering Search. 1987
Thoughts to Consider For Newly Searching Adoptees. 1987

Subject Headings:
Adoption
Birthparents
Single parents

[44]
COUNCIL FOR EXCEPTIONAL CHILDREN
1920 Association Drive
Reston, VA 22091-1589
(703) 620-3660 Voice and TDD
(703) 264-9494 Fax

History and Goals: Established in 1922, the CEC is devoted to the improvement of special education. Among its roles is the delivery of information, both printed and online, through the CEC Information Center.

Titles:

Ensuring Appropriate Services to Children and Youth with Emotional/Behavioral Disorders. 1994
Exceptional Child Education Resources. Quarterly
Exceptional Children. Bimonthly
Guiding the Social and Emotional Development of Gifted Youth: A Practical Guide for Educators and Counselors. 1992
How to Reach and Teach ADD/ADHD Children: Practical Techniques, Strategies, and Interventions for Helping Children with Attention Problems and Hyperactivity. 1993
Resourcing: Handbook for Special Education Resource Teachers. 1992
Teaching Exceptional Children. Quarterly
Teaching Gifted Kids in the Regular Classroom. 1992

Subject Headings:
Children
Education

[45]
COUNCIL ON SOCIAL WORK EDUCATION
1600 Duke Street, Suite 300
Alexandria, VA 22314-3421
(703) 683-8080
(703) 683-8099 Fax

History and Goals: This nonprofit national organization was founded in 1952 and is recognized as the sole accrediting agency for social work education in the United States. CSWE provides national leadership and a collective voice in ensuring quality social work educational programs. Two main goals are to prepare competent human service professionals and to develop new programs to meet the demands of changing service delivery systems. They sponsor an annual conference and an annual membership meeting.

Titles:
Building the Undergraduate Social Work Library: An Annotated Bibliography. Rev. ed. 1993
Journal of Social Work Education. Triannual
Social Work Education and Public Human Services, Developing Partnerships. 1993
Social Work Education Reporter. Triannual
Social Work in Rural Communities. 2nd ed. 1993
Statistics on Social Work Education in the United States. Annual
Summary Information on Master of Social Work Programs. Annual

Subject Headings:
Human services
Social service
Social work education

[46]
COUNCIL ON SOCIAL WORK EDUCATION COMMISSION ON GAY MEN AND LESBIAN WOMEN
1600 Duke Street, Suite 300
Alexandria, VA 22314-3421
(703) 683-8080
(703) 683-8099 Fax

History and Goals: Founded in 1988, The Council of Social on Social Work Education Commission on Gay Men and Lesbian Women develops, reviews, and assesses curriculum materials in relation to gay and lesbian content. The Commission plans and carries out educational programs at the annual conference of Council on Social Work Education (CSWE) and consults with social work programs and other CSWE commissions and committees on addressing the needs of sexual minorities through social work education.

Titles:
An Annotated Bibliography of Gay and Lesbian Readings for Social Workers, Other Helping Professionals and Consumers of Services. 1991
Lesbian & Gay Lifestyles: A Guide for Counseling & Education. 1992

Subject Headings:
Gays
Homosexuality
Lesbians

[47]

ETHICS AND PUBLIC POLICY CENTER

1015 15th Street, NW, Suite 900
Washington, DC 20005
(202) 682-1200
(202) 408-0632 Fax

History and Goals: Founded in 1976, the Center has a program of research, writing, publications and conferences whose purpose is to emphasize the importance of the relationship between Judeo-Christian moral values and the formation of domestic and international public policy decisions. The organization recognizes those who demonstrate integrity, morality, and ethical values in making their decisions.

Titles:

American Character. Quarterly
American Jews and the Separationist Faith. 1992
American Purpose. 10/year
Being Christian Today. 1992
Ethics and Public Policy Center Newsletter. Quarterly
Might and Right After the Cold War. 1993
No Longer Exiles: The Religious New Right in America. 1993
Points of Light: New Approaches to Ending Welfare Dependency. 1991
Racial Preferences and Racial Justice: The New Affirmative Action Policy. 1991

Subject Headings:
Ethics
Public policy

[48]

FAMILIES INTERNATIONAL, INC.

11700 West Lake Park Drive
Milwaukee, WI 53224
(414) 359-1040
(800) 852-1944 (Publications only)
(414) 359-1074 Fax

History and Goals: Families International, Inc., is a nonprofit international agency dedicated to strengthening family life through its community based support system of services and counseling. The organizational goal is to assist individuals and families in solving a variety of problems. This is accomplished by supporting the efforts of its network of member agencies which is carried out by its service arm, Family Service America, Inc.. The Agency sponsors: research reports; technical assistance; national programs; and the Severson National Information Center, a national clearinghouse on family issues.

Titles:

AIDS: A Complete Guide to Psychosocial Intervention. 1992
Assessment: A Sourcebook For Social Work Practice. 1993
Crisis Intervention, Book 2: The Practitioner's Sourcebook for Brief Therapy. 1990
Directory of Member Agencies. 1994
Empowering Hispanic Families. 1991
Families in Society. 10/year
Family. 1990

From Issue to Action: An Advocacy Program Model. 1991
Garrett's Interviewing: Its Principles and Method. 1995
Rebuilding the Nest: A New Commitment to the American Family. 1990
Psychosocial and Policy Issues in the World of Work. 1995
The State of Families. Serial

Subject Headings:
Family

[49]
FAMILIES U.S.A. FOUNDATION
1334 G Street NW, Suite 300
Washington, DC 20005
(202) 628-3030
(202) 347-2417 Fax
Internet Site: http://epn.org/fam-usa.html

History and Goals: Families USA, originally known as the Villers Foundation, was founded by Phillippe Villers in 1981 both as a grant-making foundation and a health care advocacy group. Their mission is to work towards reforming the health care system in the United States so that universal access to health care is assured for all Americans.

Titles:
Families USA Guide to the U.S. Congress. 1993
How Americans Lose Health Insurance. 1994
The Human Impact of Health Reform: Clinton vs Cooper vs Chafee. 1994
Losing Health Insurance: Two Million Americans Each Month. 1993
More for Less: An Analysis of Health Benefits and Health Savings Under the Clinton Reform. 1994
National Health Care: An American Priority. 1990
Real Life Poverty: Where the American Public Would Set the Poverty Line. 1990
SeniorWatch. Monthly

Subject Headings:
Family
Medical care
Poverty

[50]
FAMILY RESEARCH COUNCIL
700 Thirteenth Street, NW, Suite 500
Washington, DC 20005
(202) 393-2100
(202) 393-2134 Fax
Internet Site: http://www.townhall.com/townhall/frc/welcome.html

History and Goals: The Family Research Council, an independent, nonprofit advocacy organization is dedicated to promoting and strengthening family issues on federal, state, and local levels. Founded in 1980 as a social policy research and educational organization, it merged with Focus on the Family, a nonprofit Christian media and counseling ministry in 1988. Since that time it has labored to promote its pro-family concerns to policy and legislative leaders.

Titles:
Blessed Are the Barren: The Social Policy of Planned Parenthood. 1991
Family Policy. Bimonthly
Focus on Family. Monthly
FRC In Focus Fact Sheets. Irregular
FRC Insight. Irregular
Free to be Family. 1992
Never Forget. 1993
Our Journey Home: What Parents Are Doing To Preserve Family Values. 1992
Outcome-Based Education: Dumbing Down America's Schools. 1994
Policy Papers. Monthly
Silent Minority: The Hidden Electoral Impact on Children. 1993
Washington Watch. Monthly

Subject Headings:
Family
Social policy

[51]
FAMILY RESOURCE COALITION
200 S. Michigan Avenue, Suite 1520
Chicago, IL 60604
(312) 341-0900
(312) 341-9631 Fax

History and Goals: Established in 1981, FRC is comprised of community-based family support organizations concerned with parenting, child development and family issues. It seeks to educate public, government and corporate leaders about the needs of families, and to provide resource and referral services to social service professionals dealing with families.

Titles:
The Basics of Family Support. 1994
Building Strong Foundations: Evaluation Strategies. 1986
FRC Connection. Bimonthly
FRC Report. Triannual
Know Your Community: A Step by Step Guide to Community Needs Assessment. 1995
Programs to Strengthen Families: A Resource Guide. 1992
Vulnerable Communities: Three Case Studies and Three Lessons Learned. 1994
Working with African American Families. 1994
Working with Teen Parents. 1985

Subject Headings:
Children
Family
Teenagers

[52]
FEDERATION OF PROTESTANT WELFARE AGENCIES
281 Park Avenue South
New York, NY 10010
(212) 777-4800
(212) 673-4085 Fax

History and Goals: Founded in 1922, the Federation of Protestant Welfare Agencies coordinates the work of more than 250 Protestant human service agencies in the New York City area. The organization provides consultation and assistance to member agencies, helping them to provide the necessary services and programs to meet the needs of their constituencies. It also provides a unified voice for making social welfare needs known to policymakers.

Titles:
Endangered and Abandoned: The Response of New York to Black and Latino Males. 1991
Entitled to Know: A Handbook on Benefits and Services to Low Income People in New York City. 1994
Federation of Protestant Welfare Agencies. Quarterly
A Model for Low-Income Communities. 1994
The No. 1 Killer of our Children. 1988

Subject Headings:
Poverty
Social service

[53]
FORD FOUNDATION
320 East 43rd Street
New York, NY 10017
(212) 573-5169
(212) 599-4584 Fax

History and Goals: Established in 1936 by Henry and Edsel Ford, the Ford Foundation supports a program of serving the welfare of society with a national and international perspective by funding institutions and organizations that seek to solve public problems. A private, nonprofit institution, the Foundation has funded individuals and institutions both nationally and internationally. The Catalog of Publication, Films, and Videos, supplies bibliographic and order information for Foundation and non-foundation publications, working papers, reports to the Foundation, and noteworthy videos, films, and radio programs.

Titles:
The Challenge of Local Feminism: Women's Movements in Global Perspective. 1995
Changing Relations: Newcomers and Established Residents in U.S. Communities. 1993
The Common Good: Social Welfare and the American Future. 1989
Ford Foundation Annual Report. Annual
Ford Foundation Report. Quarterly
Innovating America. 1990
Innovations in State and Local Government. Annual
Reproductive Health: A Strategy for the 1990's. 1991
Violence Against Women: Addressing a Global Problem. 1992

Subject Headings:
Public welfare
Social policy

[54]

GAY AND LESBIAN PARENTS COALITION INTERNATIONAL
P.O. Box 50360
Washington, DC 20091
(202) 583-8029
(202) 783-6204 Fax

History and Goals: Started in 1979, GLPCI links a network of local gay and lesbian parents and parent support groups, and acts as a clearinghouse for information about gay and lesbian parenting. It supports passage of legislation created to eliminate discrimination due to sexual orientation, and seeks to educate the public about the special concerns of gay and lesbian parents.

Titles:
A Bibliography on Gay and Lesbians and Their Families. 1992
Books for Children of Lesbian and Gay Parents. 1993
Gay and Lesbian Parents Coalition International—Network. Quarterly
The Lesbian and Gay Parenting Handbook: Creating and Raising Our Families. 1993
Network. Quarterly

Subject Headings:
Gay parents
Lesbian mothers
Parenting

[55]

GROUP FOR THE ADVANCEMENT OF DOCTORAL EDUCATION IN SOCIAL WORK
Columbia University
School of Social Work
622 West 113th Street
New York, NY 10025
(212) 854-5189

History and Goals: The GADE is comprised of a group of social work educators whose purpose is the advancement of doctoral education in the area of social work and to provide information on the social work doctoral programs currently in existence in the United States.

Titles:
Program Guide. 1993

Subject Headings:
Social work education

[56]

HAZELDEN FOUNDATION
15245 Pleasant Valley Road
P.O. Box 11
Center City, MN 55012-0011
(612) 257-4010
(612) 257-5101 Fax

History and Goals: This Foundation was established in 1949. They publish print and non-print information on inpatient and outpatient facilities for chemically dependent individuals; aftercare therapy, employee assistance, research, and offer other rehabilitation, education, and professional services.

Titles:

Chemically Dependent Older Adults: How Do We Treat Them? 1990

Days of Healing, Days of Joy: Daily Meditations for Adult Children. 1992

Dual Disorders Recovery Book. 1993

Final Grant Report: Chemical Abuse Among Older Women, Older Adults, and Disabled People. 1990

Understanding Depressions and Addiction. 1994

Understanding Posttraumatic Stress Disorder and Addiction. 1994

Subject Headings:

Dual diagnosis

Employee assistance programs

Substance abuse

[57]

HEMLOCK SOCIETY

P.O. Box 11830

Eugene, OR 97440-4030

(503) 342-5748

(503) 345-2751 Fax

Internet Site: http://www.irsociety.com/hemlock.html

History and Goals: Established in 1980, the Society is a national organization supporting the rights of terminally ill people to self-determination for all end-of-life decisions. The Society advocates physical-assisted dying as an option for the terminally ill. The Society's activities include education, legal and legislative activity, crisis intervention, and dissemination of information.

Titles:

Death and Dignity: Making Choices and Taking Charge. 1993

Dying In Prison: Counseling the Terminal Inmate. 1991

Euthanasia: Help With a Good Death. 1991

Final Choices: To Live or Die in an Age of Medical Technology. 1993

Final Exit: The Practicalities of Self-Deliverance and Assisted Suicide for the Dying. 1991

Hemlock News. Monthly

Hemlock Quarterly. Quarterly

Let Me Die Before I Wake: How Dying People End Their Suffering. 1992

Life's Dominion: An Argument About Abortion, Euthanasia and Individual Freedom. 1993

Right to Die: Understanding Euthanasia. 1990

Timelines. Bimonthly

Subject Headings:

Death

Euthanasia

Terminal care

[58]

HISPANIC POLICY DEVELOPMENT PROJECT

1001 Connecticut Avenue NW, Suite 538
Washington, DC 20036
(202) 822-8414
(202) 822-9120 Fax

History and Goals: HPDP is a nonprofit organization devoted to the analysis and evaluation of public policies affecting Hispanics in the United States. Special efforts are directed at the problems of Hispanic youth in the areas of education, employment, and family. HPDP also sponsors conferences and seminars, and support the work of Hispanic organizations through its research and policy studies.

Titles:

Hispanic Almanac. 3rd ed. 1993.
HPDP Research Bulletin. Quarterly
In Their Own Words: CEO Views of the Diversity At the Top. 1994
Together is Better. 1990
Too Late to Patch: Reconsidering Second-Chance Opportunities for Hispanic and Other Dropouts. 1988

Subject Headings:
Education
Hispanic Americans

[59]

HOUSING ASSISTANCE COUNCIL

1025 Vermont Avenue, NW, Suite 606
Washington, DC 20005
(202) 842-8600
(202) 347-3441 Fax

History and Goals: HAC was created in 1971 to increase the availability of decent housing for rural low-income people. The Council provides seed money loans, technical assistance, program and policy analysis, research and demonstration projects, training, and information services to public, nonprofit, and private organizations.

Titles:

Addressing Homelessness in Rural Communities. 1991
A Guide to Federal Housing and Community Development Programs for Small Towns and Rural Areas. 1994
A Guide to Housing Organizations for Rural Areas. 1992
HAC News. Biweekly
State Action Memorandum. Bimonthly

Subject Headings:
Housing
Poverty
Urban policy

[60]
HUD USER

P.O. Box 6091
Rockville, MD 20850
(800) 245-2691
(301) 251-5747 Fax
Internet Site: http://huduser.aspensys.com:84/

History and Goals: The U.S. Department of Housing and Urban Development, Office of Policy Development and Research established this information clearinghouse in 1978. The primary aim of HUD USER is to collect and disseminate information and research findings concerning housing and community development to all interested parties. This organization provides a newsletter, resource guides blueprints, referrals, software, audiovisual services, and database services.

Titles:
Creating Community: Integrating Elderly and Severely Mentally Ill Persons in Public Housing. 1993
Directory of Information Resources in Housing and Urban Development. 3rd ed. 1993
Entrepreneurial Approach to Funding Social Services: The Story of Pioneer Human Services. 1992
Public Housing Child Care Demonstration Program: Program Assessment, First Round. 1992
Recent Research Results. Monthly
Removing Regulatory Barriers to Affordable Housing: How States and Localities Are Moving Ahead. 1993

Subject Headings:
Community development
Housing

[61]
HUMAN RIGHTS WATCH

485 Fifth Avenue
New York, NY 10017
(212) 972-8400
(212) 972-0905 Fax
Internet Site: http://www.charities.org/watch.html

History and Goals: Founded in 1987, Human Rights Watch is composed of five regional divisions: Africa Watch, Americas Watch, Asia Watch, Helsinki Watch, and Middle East Watch, plus four thematic projects: the Arms Project, Prison Project, Women's Rights Project, and the Fund for Free Expression. Human Rights Watch conducts regular, systematic investigations of human rights abuses in approximately seventy countries around the world. The Watch addresses the human rights practices of governments, geopolitical alignments, and ethnic and religious persuasions.

Titles:
Denying Ethnic Identity. 1994
Final Justice: Police and Death Squad Homicides of Adolescents in Brazil. 1994
Haiti: Human Rights After President Aristide's Return. 1995
Human Rights Violations in the United States. 1994
Human Rights Watch Global Report on Women's Human Rights. 1995
Human Rights Watch Quarterly Newsletter. Periodic
Human Rights Watch World Report. Annual

Subject Headings:

Ethics
Foreign policy
Prisoners

[62]
INDEPENDENT SECTOR

1828 L Street, NW
Washington, DC 20036
(202) 223-8100
(202) 416-0580 Fax

History and Goals: Independent Sector was founded in 1980 for the purpose of serving as a national forum to develop, support and increase the commitment of volunteering among Americans. Included in the goals of the organization are the achievement of greater public awareness of volunteering, effective governmental relationships, research, increasing financial support for social concerns, and the support of excellence in the leadership of voluntary organizations.

Titles:

America's Voluntary Spirit. 1983
Building Community. 1991
Giving and Volunteering in the US. 1992
Immeasurable Returns. Quarterly
Nonprofit Almanac 1992–1993: Dimensions of the Independent Sector. 1992
The Nonprofit Lobbying Guide. 1991
Nonprofit Organizations as Private Actors. 1995
Senior Citizens as Volunteers. 1994
State Tax Trends for Nonprofits. Quarterly.

Subject Headings:

Voluntarism

[63]
INSTITUTE FOR RESEARCH ON POVERTY

University of Wisconsin - Madison
1180 Observatory Drive
3412 Social Science Building
Madison, WI 53706
(608) 262-6358
(608) 265-3119 Fax

History and Goals: Founded in 1966 at the University of Wisconsin at Madison by the United States Office of Economic Opportunity, The Institute for Research on Poverty is a university based national, nonprofit, nonpartisan research center whose purpose is to investigate the reasons and results, trends and policies of poverty, and related issues in the United States.

Titles:

Assessing the Long-term Effects of Foster Care: A Research Synthesis. 1993
Child Support Enforcement for Teenage Fathers: Problems and Prospects. 1994

The Dynamics of Homelessness. 1994

The Health, Earnings Capacity, and Poverty of Single-Mother Families. 1993

Interstate Variation in Welfare Benefits and the Migration of the Poor: Substantive Concerns and Symbolic Responses. 1994

Trends in the Size of the Nation's Homeless Population During the 1980s: A Surprising Result. 1994

What Fathers Say About Involvement with Children After Separation. 1994

Subject Headings:

Poverty

Research

[64]
INSTITUTE FOR SOCIAL RESEARCH

University of Michigan

P.O. Box 1248

Ann Arbor, MI 48106-1248

(313) 764-8363

(313) 764-2377 Fax

Internet Site: http://www.isr.umich.edu/

History and Goals: Founded in 1948, the Institute for Social Research, using three research centers (Survey Research Center, Research Center for Group Dynamics and Center for Political Studies), conducts studies, based primarily on interview surveys, of the social science aspects of both national and international populations. The organization maintains a data archive of their material which is made available to researchers.

Titles:

ISR Newsletter. Triennial

Motivation and Economic Mobility. 1985

Public Opinion and Policy Leadership in the American States. 1994

Research on the Quality of Life. 1986

The Subjective Well-Being of Young Adults: Trends and Relationships. 1988

Subject Headings:

Poverty

Research

Social service

[65]
INSTITUTE FOR WOMEN'S POLICY RESEARCH

1400 20th St., NW, Suite 104

Washington, DC 10036

(202) 785-5100

(202) 833-4362 Fax

History and Goals: Founded in 1987, The Institute examines the causes and consequences of women's poverty. They concentrate on minority women, the costs of benefits of family work policies, pay equity, wages and employment opportunities, the impact of tax policy on women and families, and access to and costs of health care.

Titles:
The Impact of the Glass Ceiling and Structural Change on Minorities and Women. 1993
Making Work Pay: The Real Employment Opportunities of Single Mothers Participating in the AFDC Program. 1994
Welfare That Works: The Working Lives of AFDC Recipients. 1995
What Do Unions Do For Women? 1994
Women and Welfare Reform: Women's Poverty, Women's Opportunities, and Women's Welfare Conference Proceedings. 1994

Subject Headings:
Poverty
Research
Single mothers

[66]
INSTITUTE ON LAW AND RIGHTS OF OLDER ADULTS
Brookdale Center on Aging of Hunter College
425 E. 25th Street
New York, NY 10010-2590
(212) 481-4433

History and Goals: The Institute was established in 1977 to ensure that the elderly poor receive access to public benefits and entitlements. The Institute offers legal support to those professionals such as social workers, attorneys, and others who are assisting the elderly. The kinds of services provided include the following: professional training, telephone case consultation, assistance at administrative hearings, public policy analysis, and conference sponsorship.

Titles:
Benefits Checklist. Annual
Entitlement Bulletin. 10/year
Help for Seniors. Bimonthly
Home Care Training Materials. 1992
Human Values and Aging Newsletter. Bimonthly
The Senior Rights Reporter. Quarterly

Subject Headings:
Aging
Gerontology

[67]
INTERAGENCY COUNCIL ON THE HOMELESS
451 Seventh Street, S.W., Suite 7274
Washington, DC 20410
(202) 708-1480

History and Goals: Established in July 1987 by the Stewart B. McKinney Homeless Assistance Act, the Council is a federal interagency group designed to deal with the homeless situation. The major activities include planning, coordinating, and monitoring programs, providing technical assistance to communities and organizations, and disseminating information on federal resources. Federal agencies and departments involved include HUD, Agriculture, Commerce, Defense, Education, Energy, Interior, Justice, Labor, Transportation, Veterans, FEMA, GSA, Postal Service, and OMB.

Titles:
Federal Programs to Help Homeless People. 1993
Outcasts on Main Street. 1993
Practical Methods for Counting Homeless People: A Manual for State and Local Jurisdictions. 1992
Reaching Out: A Guide for Service Providers. 1991
Working to End Homelessness: A Manual for States. 1991

Subject Headings:
Homelessness
Mentally ill

[68]
LAMBDA LEGAL DEFENSE AND EDUCATION FUND
666 Broadway, Suite 1200
New York, NY 10012-2317
(212) 995-8585
(212) 995-2306 Fax
Internet Site: http://nether.net/~rod/html/sub/marriage/lldef.html

History and Goals: Through test-case litigation and public education, Lambda works nationally to defend and extend the rights of lesbians, gay men, and people with HIV in areas including education, employment, housing, child custody, health care delivery, and social services delivery. Lambda Legal Defense and Education Fund is a nonprofit, tax-exempt organization founded in 1973.

Titles:
Anti-Gay Initiatives: The Pre-election Challenges. 1994
Co-Parent Rights Packet: Issues and Court Briefs. 1994
Employment Rights of Lesbian and Gay Men. 1993
HIV and Family Law: A Survey. 1994
Lambda Update. Triannual
Life Planning: Legal Documents and Protections for Lesbians and Gay Men. 1994
Negotiating for Equal Employment Benefits. 1994
OUT on the Job, OUT of a Job: A Lawyer's Overview of the Employment Rights of Lesbians and Gay Men. 1994
Sexual Orientation, HIV/AIDS, and Immigration Issues. 1994

Subject Headings:
Gays
Homosexuality
Lesbians

[69]

LEARNING DISABILITIES ASSOCIATION OF AMERICA
4156 Library Road
Pittsburgh, PA 15234
(412) 341-1515
(412) 344-0224 Fax

History and Goals: Formerly called the Association for Children with Learning Disabilities, this Association was founded in 1964 to promote education for children with learning disabilities. Through state and local chapters, the Association provides direct services and information to parents and children. The Association's major activities include research, information and referral, legal assistance, advocacy and legislative assistance, early detection and special education programs, and public awareness programs. The central office provides information and referral services to the general public.

Titles:
Advocacy Manual: A Parents' How-to Guide for Special Education Services. 1992
Attention Deficit Disorders and Hyperactivity. 6th ed. 1993
*Better Understanding Learning Disabilities: New Views from Research and Their Implications for
     Education and Public Policies.* 1993
The College Student with a Learning Disability: A Handbook. 1993
Frames of Reference for the Assessment of LD. 1994
LD in Adulthood: Persisting Problems and Evolving Issues. 1994
LDA Newsbriefs. Bimonthly
Learning Disabilities. Semiannual
Learning Disabilities and the Workplace. 1993
A Learning Disabilities Digest for Literacy Providers. 1994
Management of Children and Adolescents with AD-HD. 3rd ed. 1992
Tutoring College Students with LD: A Training Manual. 1993
What Every Parent Wants to Know—Attention Deficit Hyperactivity Disorder. 1994
When Learning is a Problem. 1992

Subject Headings:
Learning disabilities

[70]

MILTON S. EISENHOWER FOUNDATION
1660 L Street, NW, Suite 200
Washington, DC 20036
(202) 429-0440
(202) 452-0169 Fax

History and Goals: Founded in 1981, the Foundation is concerned with improving the conditions for inner-city youth and reducing drug and crime related violence. The Foundation acts as an intermediary between organizations to facilitate public advocacy, financial assistance to various neighborhood and nonprofit organizations, self-help programs, international exchange programs, and providing employment and education opportunities for youth. The Foundation has a primary interest in reaching high-risk youth and providing them with viable options to dropping out of school or turning to drugs and crime.

Titles:
Evaluating Small Scale Community Based Programs. 1995
Investing in Children and Youth. 1993
Youth Investment and Community Reconstruction. 1990

Subject Headings:
Community development
Youth

[71]
NATIONAL ALLIANCE TO END HOMELESSNESS
1518 K Street, NW, Suite 206
Washington, DC 20005
(202) 638-1526
(202) 638-4664 Fax

History and Goals: Founded in 1983, this national nonprofit organization is dedicated to the principle that no individual in American should be homeless. To this end, members of the Alliance have provided the leaders to coordinate the efforts of individuals and organizations from the private, public, and nonprofit sector to end homelessness through the implementation of policies and programs. Formerly known as the National Citizen Committee for Food and Shelter (1984) and Committee for Food and Shelter (1988), Alliance members are committed to seeking solutions that will reduce and prevent homelessness in America.

Titles:
Alliance. 11/year
Recycling for Homeless People. 1991
What Corporations Can Do to Help End Homelessness. 1990
What You Can Do to Help the Homeless. 1991

Subject Headings:
Homelessness

[72]
NATIONAL ASSEMBLY OF NATIONAL VOLUNTARY HEALTH AND SOCIAL WELFARE ORGANIZATIONS, INC.
1319 F Street NW, Suite 601
Washington, DC 20004
(202) 347-2080
(202) 393-4517 Fax

History and Goals: An association of national voluntary health and human service organizations. Through member collaboration and networking, the Assembly provided opportunities for the ongoing development of skills needed to effectively lead and manage national organizations. Members must be tax-exempt nonprofit national organizations with programs that relate to health, social welfare, and human service delivery. The organization works to advance the effectiveness of members and provides collective leadership in the areas of health and human services. It promotes public policies, programs and the development of resources which are responsive to health and human service organizations and those they serve. The Assembly helps increase public understanding of the importance of meeting human needs and furthers the development of a high quality workforce within health and human service organizations.

Titles:

Building Resiliency: What Works. 1994
The Community Collaboration Manual. 1991
Criminal History Record Checks. 1991
Directory of Internships in Youth Development. 1994
Management Compensation Report: Voluntary Health and Human Service Organizations. 1993
National Child Protection Act of 1993 (P.L. 103–209): A Legislative History. 1994
A Study in Excellence: Management in the Nonprofit Human Services. 1989
Welfare Reform Principles. 1993

Subject Headings:

Human services
Public welfare
Social policy

[73]

NATIONAL ASSOCIATION FOR CHILDREN OF ALCOHOLICS

11426 Rockville Pike, Suite 100
Rockville, MD 20852
(301) 468-0985
(301) 468-0987 Fax

History and Goals: This Association was founded in 1983. They provide educational information and advocacy services to children of alcoholics (COA) and the public at large. One goal is to increase awareness of the special needs of COA's. They also create networks in order to exchange resources and information.

Titles:

Children of Alcoholics Handbook. 1985
It's Elementary: Meeting the Needs of High-Risk Youth in the School Setting. 1989
Network. Bimonthly

Subject Headings:

Alcoholism
Children of alcoholics
Substance abuse

[74]

NATIONAL ASSOCIATION FOR COMMUNITY HEALTH CENTERS

1330 New Hampshire Avenue, NW, Suite 122
Washington, DC 20036
(202) 659-8008
(202) 659-8519 Fax

History and Goals: This organization was founded in 1970 with the mission of improving health care policies and access to health care for uninsured and the underserved populations of the U.S. NACHC regularly holds conferences, provides education, training, and technical assistance, disseminates information, conducts research, provides shared services, monitors, and lobbies Congress at the policy level, and functions as an information clearinghouse. These activities are partially funded by the federal government, but NACHC also relies on grants and membership dues to maintain operations.

Titles:

Community Health Centers: A Working Bibliography. 1991
Health Care Access and Equality: The Story of Community and Migrant Health Centers and their National Associations. 1990
Improving Access to Care for Hard-to-Reach Populations. 1992

Subject Headings:
Medical care

[75]
NATIONAL ASSOCIATION OF BLACK SOCIAL WORKERS (NABSW)
15231 W. MacNichol
Detroit, MI 48235
(313) 862-6700

History and Goals: Established in 1968, the organizational goals are to sponsor community welfare projects and programs serving the interests of the Black community.

Titles:

Preserving African American Families: Research and Action Beyond Rhetoric. 1992
Black Caucus. Quarterly

Subject Headings:
Afro Americans
Social workers

[76]
NATIONAL ASSOCIATION OF HOMES AND SERVICES FOR CHILDREN (NAHSC)
1701 K Street NW, Suite 200
Washington, DC 20006
(202) 223-3447
(202) 331-7476 Fax

History and Goals: The NAHSC was founded in 1975. The Association is the largest nation-wide membership association of private not-for-profit child and family serving organizations. It provides accreditation, advocacy and education, training, information publications, and agency support to its members.

Titles:

Caring. Quarterly
The Insider. Monthly

Subject Headings:
Children
Family

[77]
NATIONAL ASSOCIATION OF LATINO ELECTED AND APPOINTED OFFICIALS
514 C Street, NE
Washington, DC 20002
(202) 546-2536
(202) 546-4121 Fax

History and Goals: The organization was established in 1978 as the National Association of Latino Appointed Democratic Officials. Their goals are to develop a leadership network dedicated to the advancement of the Hispanic people and to articulate Hispanic needs in Washington, DC and throughout the Southwest.

Titles:

Citizenship Quarterly. Quarterly

First National Conference on Latino Children in Poverty: Proceedings. 1987

National Directory of Citizenship Services. Annual

National Roster of Hispanic Elected Officials. Annual

Naturalization Quarterly. Quarterly

Organizing a U.S. Citizenship Workshop in Your Community. 1991

Politica. Bimonthly

Surge of Naturalization in the 1990s. 1994

Unrepresentative Federal Employment Practices and Their Costs to the Hispanic Community. 1992

Subject Headings:

Hispanic Americans

[78]
NATIONAL ASSOCIATION OF SOCIAL WORKERS

750 First Street, NE, Suite 700
Washington, DC 20002-4241
(202) 408-8600
(202) 336-8312 Fax

History and Goals: The organization's purposes are to create professional standards for social work practice, advocate sound public social policies through political and legislative action, and provide a wide range of services to social workers including continuing education opportunities.

Titles:

Encyclopedia of Social Work. 19th ed. 1995

NASW News. 10/year

Social Work. Bimonthly

Social Work Abstracts. Quarterly

Social Work Almanac. 2nd ed., 1995

Social Work Dictionary. 3rd ed., 1995

Social Work in Education. Quarterly

Social Work Research. Quarterly

Social Work Speaks: NASW Policy Statements. 3rd ed. 1994

Subject Headings:

Social service
Social workers

[79]
NATIONAL ASSOCIATION OF SOCIAL WORKERS NATIONAL COMMITTEE ON LESBIAN AND GAY ISSUES

750 First Street, NE, Suite 700
Washington, DC 20002-4241
(202) 408-8600
(202) 336-8310 Fax

History and Goals: In 1977 the National Association of Social Workers Delegate Assembly adopted the Public Policy statement on Gay Issues. In 1979 the NASW Task Force on Lesbian and Gay Issues was appointed. By 1982 this committee was created as a standing unit of the association. In 1993 the NASW Delegate Assembly passed an amendment to make the National Committee on Lesbian and Gay Issues (NCOLGI) a by-laws mandated committee effective July 1994. NCOLGI proposes policy, reviews publications, identifies issues, keeps the NASW abreast regarding racial, domestic, and antigay violence and legislation. It seeks to assure equal employment opportunity for lesbians and gays and advises the national leadership and state chapters regarding lesbian and gay persons.

Titles:
Lesbian and Gay Issues: A Resource Manual for Social Workers. 1985
We're Out For You. Brochure

Subject Headings:
Gays
Homosexuality
Lesbians

[80]
NATIONAL ASSOCIATION OF STATE BUDGET OFFICERS
Hall of the States
400 N. Capitol Street, NM #295
Washington, DC 20001
(202) 624-5382
(301) 498-3738 to order publications
(202) 624-7745 Fax

History and Goals: Founded in 1945, the association's mission is to encourage study and research in state budgeting and to promote cooperation and efficiency in budget programs. They conduct educational seminars and legislative briefings.

Titles:
Budget Processes in the States. 1995
Debt Management Practices in the States. 1994
Expenditure Report. Annual
Fiscal Survey of the States. Semiannual
NASBO Directory of State Budget Offices. Semiannual
NASBO News. Bimonthly
Restructuring and Innovations in State Management: Some Recent Examples. 1993

Subject Headings:
Fiscal policy

[81]
NATIONAL ASSOCIATION OF THE DEAF
814 Thayer Avenue
Silver Spring, MD 20910-4500
(301) 587-1788
(301) 587-1791 Fax
Internet Site: http://www.charities.org/deaf.html

History and Goals: NAD is a national organization which was founded in 1880 and is devoted to dealing with issues of the deaf and hard of hearing and promoting their causes. Its primary goal is to assure a comprehensive, coordinated system of services accessible to all persons with hearing impairments thus enabling them to achieve their maximum potential. The kinds of programs and services NAD provides include information and referral, advocacy and legal assistance, grant funding, sponsorship of youth programs, national forums, conferences, publications, and information dissemination.

Titles:
The Deaf American. 8/year
Deafness—1993–2013. 1993
Deafness: Life and Culture. 1994
Junior NAD Newsletter. 7/year
NAD Broadcasters. 11/year

Subject Headings:
Deafness

[82]
NATIONAL BLACK CHILD DEVELOPMENT INSTITUTE
1023 15th Street, NW, Suite 600
Washington, DC 20005
(202) 387-1281
(202) 234-1738 Fax

History and Goals: Founded in 1970, NBCDI is dedicated to improving the quality of life for Black children and their families and focuses primarily on issues and services that fall within health, child welfare, education, and child care/early childhood education. NBCDI monitors public policy issues that affect black children and educates the public by publishing periodic reports and newsletters.

Titles:
Black Child Advocate. Quarterly
Child Health Talk. Quarterly
Guidelines for Adoption Service to Black Families and Children. 1987
Parental Drug Abuse and African American Children in Foster Care. 1991
Spirit of Excellence: Resources for Black Children Ages Three to Seven. 1991
Status of African-American Children: Twentieth Anniversary Report, 1970–1990.
Who Will Care When Parent's Can't: A Study of Black Children in Foster Care. 1989

Subject Headings:
Afro Americans
Children
Social service

[83]
NATIONAL CENTER FOR CHILDREN IN POVERTY
Columbia University School of Public Health
154 Haven Avenue
New York, NY 10032
(212) 927-8793
(212) 927-9162 Fax
Internet Site: http://cpmcnet.columbia.edu/research/campus/camp076.html

History and Goals: The NCCP was established in 1989 at the School of Public Health, Columbia University. Its goals are to strengthen programs and policies for children and their families who live in poverty in the United States through interdisciplinary analysis and dissemination of information about public and private initiative in the areas of maternal and child health, family support, and early childhood care and education.

Titles:

Alive and Well? A Research and Policy Review of Health Programs for Poor Young Children. 1991

Caring Prescriptions: Comprehensive Health Care Strategies for Young Children in Poverty. 1993

Child Care Choices, Consumer Education, and Low-Income Families. 1992

Child Poverty: A Deficit that Goes Beyond Dollars. 1994

Children and Youth: An Action Agenda. 1994

Children in Poverty: A Program Report on the First Five Years 1989–1993. 1994

Directory of Family Day Care Programs with a Low-income Focus. 1993

Five Million Children: A Statistical Profile of Our Poorest Young Children. 1990 with annual updates

Five Million Children: Data Sourcebook. 1990

In the Neighborhood: Programs That Strengthen Family Day Care for Low-Income Families. 1993

Integrating Services Integration: An Overview of Initiatives, Issues, and Possibilities. 1992

A New Way to Fight Child Poverty and Welfare Dependence: The Child Support Assurance System (CSAS). 1992

News and Issues. Tri-annual

Urban Poverty Database Inventory. 1992

Welfare Reform Seen From a Children's Perspective. 1995

Subject Headings:
Children
Poverty

[84]
NATIONAL CENTER FOR ECONOMIC ALTERNATIVES
2040 S Street, SW
Washington, DC 20009
(202) 483-6667
(202) 986-7938 Fax

History and Goals: Founded in 1977, the NCEA emerged from an effort led by the John Hay Witney Foundation and the Stern Fund. The organization conducts research and policy development projects in cooperation with foundations, federal agencies, state governments, and private nonprofit organizations. Its focus is on individual economic creativity and how different groups and individuals can best deal with special problems of race, gender, and physical disability.

Titles:

Index of Environmental Trends: An Assessment of Twenty-One Key Environmental Indicators in Nine Industrialized Countries Over the Past Two Decades. 1995

Subject Headings:
Economics
Public policy

[85]
NATIONAL CENTER FOR JUVENILE JUSTICE
710 Fifth Avenue, 3rd Fl.
Pittsburgh, PA 15219
(412) 227-6950
(412) 227-6955 Fax

History and Goals: Established in 1973, the Center is a private nonprofit organization and research division of the National Council of Juvenile and Family Court Judges. The organization's goal is to provide objective, factual information while maintaining a politically and socially neutral stance to juvenile justice practitioners at all levels. The center is dedicated to quality research in the juvenile justice field and the subsequent enhancement of juvenile justice issues on a nationwide basis.

Titles:
Cross-Cultural Research on Juvenile Justice: Proceedings of First International Forum on Youth. 1992
Fundamental Skills Training Curriculum for Juvenile Probation Officers. 1993
Guide to the Data Sets in the National Juvenile Court Data Archive. 1989
Juvenile Court Statistics. Annual
Juvenile Offenders and Victims: A Focus on Violence. 1995
Juvenile Offenders and Victims: A National Report. 1995
Juveniles and Drugs: A Review of Policy Recommendations. 1991
Kindex: An Index to Legal Periodical Literature Concerning Children. Annual
Manual for Developing a Substance Abuse Screening Protocol for the Juvenile Court and Implementing the Client Substance Index-Short Form. 1993
National Center for Juvenile Justice Annual Report 1973–1993: Twenty Years for Justice. 1994
Organization and Administration of Juvenile Services: Probation, Aftercare, and State Delinquent Institutions. 1993
Policy Alternatives and Current Court Practice in the Special Problem Areas of Jurisdiction Over the Family. 1993
Special Report on Adolescent Sex Offenders. 1992
Special Report on Juvenile Crack Dealers. 1992
State of Juvenile Probation 1992: Results of a Nationwide Survey. 1993
Today's Delinquent. Annual

Subject Headings:
Juvenile corrections
Youth

[86]
NATIONAL CENTER FOR MISSING AND EXPLOITED CHILDREN
2101 Wilson Blvd.
Suite 550
Arlington, VA 22201
(703) 235-3900
(800) 843-5678
(703) 235-4067 Fax
Internet Site: http://www.missingkids.org/

History and Goals: Founded in 1984, the NCMEC aids parents and law enforcement agencies in preventing child exploitation and in locating missing children. It serves as a national clearinghouse of information on effective state and federal legislation directed at the protection of children.

Titles:
An Analysis of Infant Abductions. 1995
Child Molesters Who Abduct. 1995
Children Traumatized in Sex Rings. 1988
Interviewing Child Victims of Sexual Exploitation. 1987
Nonprofit Service Provider's Handbook. 1990
Selected State Legislation. 2nd ed. 1989

Subject Headings:
Child welfare

[87]

NATIONAL CENTER FOR NONPROFIT BOARDS
2000 L Street, NW
Suite 510
Washington, DC 20036-4907
(202) 452-6262
(202) 452-6299 Fax

History and Goals: Formed in 1988 to advance the effectiveness of the governing boards of American nonprofit organizations, the Center offers programs, workshops, and services to board members, directors, development directors, and other nonprofit staff.

Titles:
Board Member. Bimonthly
The Board's Role in Effective Volunteer Involvement. 1995
Developing the Nonprofit Board. 1994
Nonprofit Governance Case Studies. 1994
Oversight or Interference? Striking a Balance in Nonprofit Governance. 1995
A Snapshot of America's Nonprofit Boards: Results of a National Survey. 1995

Subject Headings:
Nonprofit organizations
Organization effectiveness

[88]

NATIONAL CENTER FOR SERVICE INTEGRATION
Information Clearinghouse on Service Integration
c/o Child & Family Policy Center
218 6th Avenue
Fleming Bldg, Suite 1021
Des Moines, IA 50309
(515) 280-9027

History and Goals: The NCSI was established by grants from private foundations and the U.S. Department of Health and Human Services. It exists to guide and support the integration of educational, health, and other human services toward needy children and their families in the United States. This mission is carried out through an information clearinghouse and a technical assistance center.

Titles:

Beyond the Buzzwords: Key Principles in Effective Frontline Practice. 1994

Case Management: An Annotated Bibliography. 1993

Charting a Course: Assessing a Community's Strengths and Needs. 1993

Directory of Federally Funded Resource Centers. 1993

Getting Started: Planning a Comprehensive Services Initiative. 1993

Making a Difference: Moving to Outcome-Based Accountability for Comprehensive Service Reforms. 1994

Making it Simpler: Streamlining Intake and Eligibility Systems. 1993

NCSI News. Biannual

Service Integration: An Annotated Bibliography. 1993

So You Think You Need Help: Making Effective Use of Technical Assistance. 1993

Who Should Know What? Confidentiality and Information Sharing in Service Integration. 1994

Subject Headings:

Family policy

Family social work

Human services

[89]

NATIONAL CENTER ON ELDER ABUSE

810 First Street, NE, Suite 500

Washington, DC 20002-4267

(202) 682-2470

(202) 289-6555 Fax

History and Goals: The National Center on Elder Abuse was established in October 1993 to replace the National Aging Resource Center in Elder Abuse. The organization is funded by a cooperative agreement grant awarded to the American Public Welfare Association by the Administration on Aging. The Center is operated by a consortium of the American Public Welfare Association, the National Association of State Units on Aging, the University of Delaware, and the National Committee for the Prevention of Elder Abuse. The mission of the organization is to develop and provide information, data and expertise to federal, state, and local agencies, professionals, and the public on a timely basis. The NCEA assists organizations and individuals in their efforts against elder abuse, neglect, and exploitation by conducting workshops, producing newsletters, operating an information clearinghouse, engaging in research, and developing and disseminating technical reports of national significance.

Titles:

Elder Abuse and Neglect: A National Research Agenda. 1991

Elder Abuse and Neglect: A Synthesis of Research. 1990

Elder Abuse in the United States: An Issue Paper. 1990

Elder Abuse Public Education. 1991

Elder Abuse: Questions and Answers. 5th ed. 1995

The Implementation Status of the New Federal Abuse Prevention Program in States: A Summary of Survey Finding. 1991

Institutional Elder Abuse: A Summary of Data Gathered from State Units on Aging, State APS Agencies, and State Long-Term Care Ombudsman Programs. 1992

Interviewing Skills to Use with Abuse Victims Who Have Developmental Disabilities. 1992

NARCEA Exchange Newsletter. Bimonthly

Summaries of National Elder Abuse Data: An Exploratory Study of State Statistics. 1990
Summaries of the Statistical Data on Elder Abuse in Domestic Settings for FY90 and FY91. 1993

Subject Headings:
Abused aged
Aged

[90]

NATIONAL CENTER ON WOMEN AND FAMILY LAW

799 Broadway, Suite 402
New York, NY 10003
(212) 674-8200
(212) 533-5104 Fax

History and Goals: The Center litigates and provides legal assistance and information to advocates, policymakers and attorneys for low-income women. The Center's emphasis is on battery, child custody, child sexual abuse, child support, parental kidnapping, and the rights of single mothers.

Titles:
The Effect of Woman Abuse on Children. 1991
A Manual for Domestic Violence Advocates. 1992
The Women's Advocate: Newsletter of the National Center on Women and Family Law. Quarterly

Subject Headings:
Abused women
Custody of children
Family violence

[91]

NATIONAL CLEARINGHOUSE FOR ALCOHOL & DRUG INFORMATION

P.O. Box 2345
Rockville, MD 20847-2345
(800) 729-6686
Internet Site: http://www.health.org/

History and Goals: The National Clearinghouse for Alcohol & Drug Information (NCADI) publishes a multitude of materials in different formats about alcohol and other drugs. NCADI is the information component of the Center for Substance Abuse Prevention, which is part of the U.S. Department of Health & Human Services.

Titles:
Alcohol Health and Research World. Serial
The Behavioral Counseling Model for Injection Drug Users. 1993
Behavioral Treatments for Drug Abuse and Dependence. 1993
Cocaine Treatment: Research and Clinical Perspectives. 1993
CSAP Prevention Pipeline. Bimonthly
CSAP Prevention Resource Guide. 1992
Diagnostic Source Book for Drug Abuse Research and Treatment. 1993
Drug Abuse Among Minority Youth: Methodological Issues and Recent Advances. 1993
Drug Abuse Treatment in Prisons and Jails. 1992
Elementary Youth. 1994
Experience with Community Action Projects: New Research in the Prevention of Alcohol and Other Drug Problems. 1993

NIDA Notes. Bimonthly
Maternal Substance Use Assessment Methods Reference Manual. 1993
Practitioners: Working With Ethnic/Racial Communities. 1992
Prevention Plus III. 1992
Rural Communities. 1994
Survey Measurement of Drug Use: Methodological Studies. 1992
Working with Youth in High Risk Environments: Experiences in Prevention. 1993

Subject Headings:
Alcohol
Drugs
Substance abuse

[92]
NATIONAL CLEARINGHOUSE FOR LEGAL SERVICES
205 W. Monroe Street, 2nd Floor
Chicago, IL 60606-5013
(312) 263-3830
(800) 621-3256
(312) 939-4536 Fax

History and Goals: The Clearinghouse is a resource center and legal research system that offers a complete source of civil poverty law publications. It also makes available information on case law with respect to issues relating to poor people. The Clearinghouse operates an extensive brief bank of cases and publications relating to poverty law and the consumer.

Titles:
Access to Emergency Medical Care: Patients' Rights and Remedies. 1991
Advocacy Program for Battered Women Training Manual. 1991
Clearinghouse Review. Monthly
Desegregating Public Housing in the 1990's Through Voluntary Affirmative Action. 1991
Directory of the National Support Centers. 1991
Establishing a Right to Housing: An Advocate's Guide. 1991
Federal Register Highlights Newsletter. Biweekly
Homeless Legal Advocates' Manual. 1992
Index to SSA Cases Decided by the US Court of Appeals for the Fourth Circuit. 1991
Training Materials on Homelessness Issues. 1991

Subject Headings:
Legal aid
Public welfare

[93]
NATIONAL CLEARINGHOUSE ON CHILD ABUSE AND NEGLECT INFORMATION
P.O. Box 1182
Washington, DC 20013-1182
(703) 385-7565
(800) 394-3366
(703) 385-3206 Fax
Internet Site: http://www.acf.dhhs.gov/acfprograms/nccan/index.html

History and Goals: The Clearinghouse is an information service of the National Center on Child Abuse and Neglect. The Clearinghouse collects and disseminates information on all aspects of child abuse and neglect by maintaining a number of databases and developing publications. Kinds of materials included are monographs, documents, audiovisual materials, program directories, and public awareness materials.

Titles:
Child Abuse and Neglect: A Shared Community Concern. 1992
Guide to Funding Resources for Child Abuse and Neglect and Family Violence Programs. 1992

Subject Headings:
Child abuse
Family violence

[94]
NATIONAL CLEARINGHOUSE ON MARITAL AND DATE RAPE
2325 Oak Street
Berkeley, CA 94708-1697
(510) 524-1582
Internet Site: http://www.emf.net/~cheetham/gna-pe-1.html

History and Goals: This organization began as the Women's History Research Center in 1968 and functioned as a nonprofit research association until 1989, when it disbanded due to a lack of funding. It quickly reformed as the for-profit NCMDR and narrowed its focus in order to concentrate on legislative issues. Today, the organization provides rape prevention education through publication sales, fee-based telephone consultations, and speaking engagements with the goal of improving rape awareness issues in the United States.

Titles:
The State Law Chart. Annual

Subject Headings:
Family violence
Rape

[95]
NATIONAL COALITION AGAINST DOMESTIC VIOLENCE
P.O. Box 18749
Denver, CO 80218-0749
(303) 839-1852
(303) 831-9251 Fax

History and Goals: Formed in 1978, this nonprofit membership organization was created with the primary goal of eliminating violence and the threat of violence from the lives of women and children. This national group represents 450 independent, community-based organizations that provide shelter and support services to abused women and children. NCADV functions as both a communication network and as an information clearinghouse. They hold national conferences, publish a quarterly newsletter, sell publications, coordinate legislative lobbying efforts, and provide technical assistance to new programs.

Titles:
A Current Analysis of the Battered Women's Movement. 1992
Guidelines for Mental Health Practitioners in Domestic Violence. 1987

National Directory of Domestic Violence Programs—A Guide to Community Shelter, Safe Home and Service Programs. 1994
NCADV Update. Quarterly
NCADV VOICE. Quarterly
Rural Resource Packet. 2nd. ed. 1991

Subject Headings:
Abused women
Child abuse
Family violence

[96]
NATIONAL COALITION FOR THE HOMELESS
1612 K Street, NW, Suite 1004
Washington, DC 20006-2802
(202) 775-1322
(202) 775-1316 Fax
(202) 775-1372 Hotline
Internet Site: http://www3.arinet/home/nch/wwwhome.html

History and Goals: The Homelessness Information Exchange merged with the National Coalition for the Homeless. The National Coalition is the parent organization and the HIE is considered a department within that organization. The National Coalition for the Homeless is a national information service offering information on programs, policies, and research related to homelessness. The Coalition works in conjunction with the HIE in educating and providing information to policymakers and the public. The kinds of information collected include demographic, program summaries, and research studies. Topics include housing, prevention, emergency and transitional shelter, mental health/medical services, job creation, education, etc. Together with HIE, the Coalition produces numerous reports and fact sheets.

Titles:
Addiction on the Streets: Substance Abuse and Homelessness in America. 1992
Closing Door: Economic Causes of Homelessness. 1990
Coalition Building to Address Homelessness. 1985
Comprehensive Planning to Address Homelessness. 1987
A Directory of Statewide and National Homeless/Housing Advocacy Organizations. 3rd ed. 1994
Essential Reference on Homelessness. 1994
Fatally Flawed: The Census Bureau's Count of Homeless People. 1991
Helping the Homeless in Your Community. 1988
Heroes Today, Homeless Tomorrow? Homelessness Among Veterans in the United States. 1991
Homeless in America: A Summary. Rev. ed. 1990
Homewords. Quarterly
Life and Death on the Streets: Health Care Reform and Homelessness. 1993
Mourning in America: Health Problems, Mortality and Homelessness. 1991
A Place Called Hopelessness. 1992
Safety Network. Bimonthly
Shredding the Safety Net: The Contract with America's Impact on Poor and Homeless People. 1994
Tis a Gift to be Simple: Homelessness, Health Care Reform, and the Single Payer Solution. 1994
Transitional Housing. 1990

Subject Headings:
Homelessness
Poverty
Urban policy

[97]
NATIONAL COALITION OF HISPANIC MENTAL HEALTH AND HUMAN SERVICES ORGANIZATIONS

1501 16th St., NW
Washington, DC 20036
(202) 387-5000

History and Goals: Founded in 1973, the Coalition claims to be the only national organization which strives to improve health and public services to Hispanics by helping Hispanic organizations develop programs. This organization also produces books and videos.

Titles:
COSSMHO Reporter. Quarterly

Subject Headings:
Hispanic Americans
Human services
Mental health

[98]
NATIONAL COMMITTEE FOR ADOPTION

1930 17th Street NW
Washington, DC 20009
(202) 328-1200

History and Goals: The organization has worked since 1980 to protect traditional adoption practices, assure confidentiality and privacy in adoption, and promote adoption regulation. The Committee generally opposes open adoption. (See also entry 101)

Titles:
Adoption Factbook. 1989
Memo. Biweekly
National Adoption Reports. Bimonthly

Subject Headings:
Adoption

[99]
NATIONAL COMMITTEE FOR PREVENTION OF CHILD ABUSE

332 S. Michigan Avenue, Suite 950
Chicago, IL 60604
(312) 663-3520
(312) 939-8962 Fax

History and Goals: Founded in 1972, NCPCA is a national volunteer organization dedicated to the prevention of child abuse. The Committee's primary activities include research, education and training, advocacy, public awareness, and national networking with similar organizations.

Titles:

Child Protection: Guidebook for Child Care Providers. 1991

Cross-Cultural Partnerships for Child Abuse Prevention with Native American Communities. 1991

Current Trends in Child Abuse Reporting and Fatalities. 1992

Physical Child Abuse. 2nd ed. 1992

Preventing Child Abuse: An Evaluation of Services to High-Risk Families. 1993

Public Opinion and Behaviors Regarding Child Abuse Protection. 1995

Selected Child Abuse Information and Resources Directory. 1992

What Every Parent Should Know. 1987

Subject Headings:
Child abuse
Family social work

[100]
NATIONAL CONFERENCE OF STATE LEGISLATURES
1560 Broadway, Suite 700
Denver, CO 80202
(303) 830-2054
(303)863-8003 Fax
Internet Site: http://www.ncsl.org/

History and Goals: NCSL services the legislators and staffs of the nation's fifty states, its commonwealths, and territories. Created in 1975, the Conference is a nonpartisan organization with three objectives: (1) to improve the quality and effectiveness of state legislatures; (2) to foster interstate communication and cooperation; (3) and to ensure states a strong, cohesive voice in the federal system.

Titles:

Adolescent Health Issues: State Actions 1992–1994. 1995

Adolescents and the HIV/AIDS Epidemic: Stemming the Tide. 1993

Adult Workers: Retraining the American Workforce. 1994

America's Newcomers: A State and Local Policymakers' Guide to Immigration and Immigrant Policy. 1993

America's Newcomers: An Immigration Policy Guide. 1994

America's Newcomers: Community Relations and Ethnic Diversity. 1994

Children Achieving Potential: An Introduction to Elementary School Counseling and State-Level Policies. 1990.

Healthy Babies: State Initiatives for Pregnant Women at Risk. 1993

Healthy Kids: State Initiatives to Improve Children's Health. 1993

Issues Outlook 1994. 1994

Learning How to Compete: Workforce Skills and State Economic Development Policies. 1995

Mandate Monitor. Monthly

State Legislative Staff Directory. 1993

State Legislatures. Monthly

1992 State Legislative Summary: Children, Youth, and Family Issues. 1992

What Legislators Need to Know About Alcohol and Other Drug Abuse. 1995

What Legislators Need to Know About Managed Care. 1994

Subject Headings:
Public policy
State governments

[101]
NATIONAL COUNCIL FOR ADOPTION
1930 Seventeenth Street, NW
Washington, DC 20009-6207
(202) 328-1200
(202) 332-0935 Fax

History and Goals: The Council, a nonprofit, nonsectarian organization, serves as a national advocate for adopted children, adoptive parents, and birth parents. Founded in 1980, the Council works to protect adopted children and ensure confidentiality of all involved parties. The Council also serves as an information clearinghouse, provides technical assistance, compiles statistics, and offers counseling services. (See also entry 98)

Titles:
Adoption Factbook. 1989
Encyclopedia of Adoption. 1991
National Adoption Reports. Quarterly

Subject Headings:
Adoption
Birthparents
Children

[102]
NATIONAL COUNCIL OF COMMUNITY MENTAL HEALTH CENTERS
12300 Twinbrook Parkway, Suite 320
Rockville, MD 20852
(301) 984-6200
(301) 881-7159 Fax

History and Goals: Founded in 1970, the National Council of Community Mental Health Centers is the oldest and largest organization representing community mental health care provider organizations and state associations across the United States. Its members support the provision of accessible, comprehensive, clinically effective, and cost-efficient mental health services. The organization tracks, responds to, and monitors legislative and regulatory developments in the area of mental health. In addition, the Organization works to support and enhance member organization's opportunities for competitive expansion in the private marketplace.

Titles:
Business Yardsticks—An Introduction to Financial Ratios. 1991
Community Mental Health Journal. Bimonthly
Contemporary Directions in Human Resource Management. 1990
Getting the Most From a Client Satisfaction Survey. 1994
National Council News. 11/year
National Registry of Community Mental Health Services. 1991
New Perspectives on Mental Healthcare in America: Exploring Windows of Opportunity. 1992
The Psychiatric Staffing Crisis in Community Mental Health. 1990
The Quality Challenge: Continuous Improvement in Behavioral Healthcare. 1993
Serving the Elderly—A Mental Health Resource Guide. 1989
Software Applications for Mental Health: A Directory and Resource Guide. 1994
Survey of Salary, Benefits and Staffing Patterns of Community Mental Health Providers. 1991
Thriving in Turbulent Times: The Challenges for Behavioral Healthcare Managers. 1993
Today's HealthCare Manager. Bimonthly

Subject Headings:
Mental health

[103]
NATIONAL COUNCIL ON ALCOHOLISM AND DRUG DEPENDENCE
12 West 21st Street, 7th Floor
New York, NY 10010
(212) 206-6770
(800) NCA-CALL
(212) 645-1690 Fax

History and Goals: Founded in 1944 as the National Council on Alcoholism, NCADD seeks to prevent the disease of alcoholism, other drug addictions, and related problems; educate the public about alcoholism, other drug addictions, and related problems; encourage research in the prevention, diagnosis, and treatment of these addictions; and advocate policies to reduce addictions and meet the treatment needs and the rights of affected individuals, families, and communities. The Council sponsors National Alcohol Awareness Month in April and National Fetal Alcohol Syndrome Awareness Week.

Titles:
Acquired Immune Deficiency Syndrome and Chemical Dependency. 1987
Alcoholism: Clinical and Experimental Research. Serial
Alcoholism Resource Directory. 1987
Alcoholism Resource Index. Loose-leaf
Defining Adolescent Alcohol Use. 1977
A Federal Response to a Hidden Epidemic: Alcohol & Other Drug Problems Among Women. 1987
Recent Developments in Alcoholism. Serial
Women, Alcohol, Other Drugs and Pregnancy. 1990

Subject Headings:
Alcoholism
Drug abuse
Substance abuse

[104]
NATIONAL COUNCIL ON CRIME AND DELINQUENCY
685 Market Street, Suite 620
San Francisco, CA 94105
(415) 896-6223
(415) 896-5109 Fax

History and Goals: NCCD was originally organized in 1907 as the National Probation Association. NCCD develops model legislation, provides professional training, conducts research, and formulates policies related to issues of crime control and corrections.

Titles:
Crime and Delinquency. Quarterly
Criminal Justice Abstracts. Serial
Does Imprisonment Reduce Crime: A Critique of "Voodoo" Criminology. 1993
Image and Reality: Juvenile Crime, Youth Violence and Public Policy. 1995
Journal of Research in Crime and Delinquency. Semiannual
Juvenile Justice: Improving the Quality of Care. 1992

The Juveniles Taken Into Custody Research Program: Estimating the Prevalence of Juvenile Custody by Race and Gender. 1993
NCCD News. Bimonthly
NCCD News Fronts. Quarterly
A New Approach to Child Protection: The CRC Model. 1993
Partnerships to Prevent Youth Violence. 1994
Prevention for a Safer Society. 1993
The "Prisons Pay" Studies: Research or Ideology. 1993
Reducing Crime in America: A Pragmatic Approach. 1993
Solving the Violence Problems: Teens, Crime and the Community. 1995
The State of the Art in Jail Drug Treatment Programs. 1994
Who Goes to Prison? 1990
Women's Prisons: Overcrowded and Overused. 1992
Youth Forum. Serial

Subject Headings:
Corrections
Crime

[105]
NATIONAL COUNCIL ON FAMILY RELATIONS
3989 Central Avenue NE, Suite 550
Minneapolis, MN 55421
(612) 781-9331
(612) 781-9348 Fax

History and Goals: Organized in 1938, the NCFR is a nonprofit organization of professionals in the areas of social work, counseling, education, psychology, sociology, etc., who work with families. It is the oldest multidisciplinary family organization in the United States.

Titles:
Contemporary Families: Looking Forward, Looking Back. 1991
Family Health: From Data to Policy. 1993
Initiatives for Families: Research, Policy, Practice and Education. 1995
Inventory of Marriage and Family Literature. Annual
Journal of Marriage and the Family. Quarterly
One World, Many Families. 1993
Teaching Family Policy: A Handbook of Course Syllabi, Teaching Strategies and Resources. 1993
Two Thousand One: Preparing Families of the Future. 1990
Vision 2010: Families and Adolescents. 1994
The Work and Family Interface: Toward a Contextual Effects Perspective. 1995

Subject Headings:
Family

[106]
NATIONAL COUNCIL ON THE AGING
409 Third Street, SW
Washington, DC 20024
(202) 479-1200
(202) 479-6674 TDD
(202) 479-0735 Fax

History and Goals: Since 1950 the NCOA has provided individuals and organizations information on services, programs, and policies in the field of aging.

Titles:

Abstracts in Social Gerontology: Current Literature on Aging. Quarterly
Adding Health to Years: A Basic Handbook on Older People's Health. 1993
Caregiver Support Groups in America. 1990
Challenges in an Aging Society. 1994
Current Literature on Aging. Quarterly
Intergenerational Relations in America: The Recognition of Interdependence. 1995
Let Us Serve Them All Their Days: Young Volunteers Serving Homebound Elderly Persons—A Handbook of Program Ideas. 1992
Long Distance Caregiving: A Survival Guide for Far Away Caregivers. 1993
Making Your Voice HEARD: An Advocacy Manual for Board Members and Staff of Programs and Services for Older Americans. 1993
NCOA Networks. Bimonthly
The New Medicine Man: A Different Kind of Health Care for Seniors. 1992
Perspective on Aging. Quarterly
Preparing for an Aging Society. 1992
Profile of Rural Older Americans. 1995

Subject Headings:
Aged
Aging
Gerontology

[107]
NATIONAL DISPLACED HOMEMAKERS NETWORK

1625 K Street NW, Suite 300
Washington, DC 20006
(202) 467-6346
(202) 467-5366 Fax

History and Goals: The NDHN was established in 1979 with the goal of assisting displaced homemakers to become economically self-sufficient. NDHN lobbies Congress and works with business leaders to create programs to aid displaced homemakers. The Network offers educational services and publications to increase awareness of the needs of the 15.6 million displaced homemakers in the U.S. The NDHN also provides information on the more than 1,100 programs, agencies and educational institutions that provide job training and other services to displaced homemakers.

Titles:

Displaced Homemaker Program Directory. Annual
Low-Wage Jobs and Workers: Trends and Options for Change. 1989
The More Things Change: A Status Report on Displaced Homemakers and Single Parents in the 1990's. 1990
Network News. Quarterly
Transition Times. Semiannual

Subject Headings:
Displaced homemakers
Single mothers

[108]
NATIONAL FEDERATION OF PARENTS AND FRIENDS OF GAYS
8020 Eastern Avenue, NW
Washington, DC 20012
(202) 726-3223

History and Goals: Founded in 1980, the National Federation of Parents & Friends of Gays (NF/PFOG) is a nonprofit organization composed of volunteer local community based counselors, peer counselors, and service providers. Through its National Resource Center & Library, NF/PFOG provides programs and services including an international directory of support services, bibliographies listing educational resource materials and recommended readings, and subject specific support packets. NF/PFOG maintains a national hotline and speakers bureau.

Titles:
Homosexuality as Viewed from Five Perspectives. 1987
International Directory. Semiannual

Subject Headings:
Gays
Homosexuality
Lesbians

[109]
NATIONAL FEDERATION OF SOCIETIES FOR CLINICAL SOCIAL WORK
P.O. Box 3740
Arlington, VA 22203
(713) 522-3866
(713) 522-9441 Fax

History and Goals: This national advocacy organization evolved from a meeting among six state societies for clinical social work in 1971. Primary goals are to promote clinical social work education, research, and publication; to support freedom of choice laws statewide and nationally; and increase the public's awareness about clinical social work. The Federation promotes ethical standards for practitioners, sponsors the Clinical Social Work Journal, and provides a newsletter to members.

Titles:
Clinical Social Work Journal. Quarterly

Subject Headings:
Social service
Social work education
Social workers

[110]
NATIONAL GAY AND LESBIAN TASK FORCE
2320 17th St., NW
Washington, DC 20009-2702
(202) 332-6483
(202) 332-0207 Fax

History and Goals: Founded in 1973, The National Gay & Lesbian Task Force (NGLTF) is the oldest national gay and lesbian civil rights advocacy and lobbying organization. It is dedicated to building a movement to promote freedom and full equality for all lesbians and gay men. The Task Force is organized into the following areas: lobbying, organization and technical assistance, public information and direct action. Increased funding for AIDS research and education and opposition to laws that discriminate against gays and people with AIDS are major lobbying efforts. Publications reflect projects and initiatives of the task force.

Titles:
Anti-Gay/Lesbian Violence, Victimization & Defamation in 1993. 1994
Activist Alert. Monthly
Bibliography of Anti-Violence Materials. 1994
Countering Right-Wing Rhetoric. 1993
Gay/Lesbian/Bisexual Civil Rights in the U.S. 1994
National Gay and Lesbian Task Force—Task Force Report. Quarterly
NGLTF Newsletter and Fact Sheet. Quarterly
Organizations Working Against Violence. 1994
Organizing Manual—Hate Crime Legislation. 1992
Pervasive Patterns of Discrimination. 1992

Subject Headings:
Gays
Homosexuality
Lesbians

[111]
NATIONAL GOVERNOR'S ASSOCIATION
444 N. Capitol Street, Suite 267
Hall of the States
Washington, DC 20001-1572
(202) 624-5300
(202) 624-5313 Fax

History and Goals: Founded in 1908, the National Governor's Association has worked together on government, policy economic, social, health, and environmental issues. Comprised of the Governors of the fifty states, the Commonwealth of the Northern Mariana Islands and Puerto Rico, the Territories of the American Samoa, Guam and the Virgin Islands, the Association meets twice annually to discuss areas of concern on national and local levels.

Titles:
Advancing America's Workforce. 1994
Changing Systems for Children and Families. 1994
Directory of Governors of American States, Commonwealths and Territories. Annual
Every Child Ready for School: Report of the Action Team on School Readiness. 1992
Fiscal Surveys of the States. Annual
Gaining Ground: State Initiatives for Pregnant Women and Children. 1992
Governor's Bulletin. Bi-Weekly
Governor's Staff Directory. Annual
A Healthy America: The Challenge for States. 1991

Measuring Access to Care. 1994
Policy Positions. Annual
Promoting Quality Business: A State Action Agenda. 1992
State Expenditure Reports. Annual
Strengthening Families: A Guide for State Policymaking. 1991
Where are the Jobs? 1994

Subject Headings:
Governors
Social policy
State governments

[112]
NATIONAL HEALTH INFORMATION CENTER
P.O. Box 1133
Washington, DC 20013-1133
(301) 565-4167
(301) 984-4256 Fax
Internet Site: http://nhic-nt.health.org/

History and Goals: The National Health Information Center is a service of the Office of Disease Prevention and Health Promotion, U.S. Public Health Service. The Center serves primarily as a health information referral service answering questions and referring people to the appropriate sources. The Center also develops publications on health-related topics of interest to health professionals, the media, and the public.

Titles:
Federal Health Information Centers and Clearinghouses. 1992
Healthy People 2000: Action Series. 1992
Healthy People 2000: Fact Sheet. 1992
Healthy People 2000: National Health and Promotion and Disease Prevention Objectives. 1991
Healthy People 2000: Resource Lists. 1992
Healthy People 2000: Specific Populations and Settings. 1992

Subject Headings:
Medical care

[113]
NATIONAL LEAGUE OF CITIES
1301 Pennsylvania Avenue NW, Suite 550
Washington, DC 20004-1763
(202) 626-3000
(202) 626-3043 Fax
Internet Site: http://pti.nw.dc.us/nlc.htm

History and Goals: Founded in 1924 as the American Municipal Association by ten state municipal leagues, it became the National League of Cities in 1964. Its members now include 49 state municipal organizations and over 1,400 communities of all sizes in every state. The original goal of the organization was to make cities efficient and to improve the delivery of municipal services. Since then the organization has moved into the area of public policy and has played an important role in shaping federal legislation and policies affecting local governments.

Titles:

All In It Together: Cities, Suburbs and Local Economic Regions. 1993

City Fiscal Conditions in 1995. 1995

A Comprehensive Guide to Studies on State and Federal Mandates to Localities: An Annotated Bibliography. 1994

Directory of City Policy Officials. Annual

Directory of Local Women Elected Officials. Annual

Global Dollars, Local Sense: Cities and Towns in the International Economy. 1993

The Information Superhighway Game. 1994

Issues and Options. 10/year

Making Government Work For Your City's Kids: Getting Through the Intergovernmental Maze of Programs for Children and Families. 1992

Minority Business Programs and Disparity Studies. 1994

Nation's Cities Weekly. Weekly

A New Agenda for Cities. 1992

Poverty and Economic Development: Views From City Hall. 1994

State of America's Cities. Annual

Urban Affairs Abstracts. Monthly

Ways and Means for Children and Families. 1991

Subject Headings:

Cities and towns

Economics

[114]
NATIONAL NETWORK FOR SOCIAL WORK MANAGERS

6501 N. Federal Hwy., Suite 5
Boca Raton, FL 33487
(407) 997-7560
(407) 241-6746 Fax

History and Goals: Founded in 1985, the Network seeks to enhance social work managers' careers in such areas as administration, management, planning, budgeting, economics, and legislative work. They conduct the National Management Institute, regional management development workshops, and other educational programs.

Titles:

Administration in Social Work. Quarterly

Annual Monograph of Papers. Annual

Managers' Choices: Compelling Issues in the New Decision Environment. 1992

Social Work Executive. Quarterly

Subject Headings:

Social service

Social work administration

Social workers

[115]
NATIONAL NETWORK OF RUNAWAY AND YOUTH SERVICES

1319 F Street, NW, Suite 401
Washington, DC 20004
(202) 783-7949
(202) 783-7955 Fax

History and Goals: The National Network of Runaway and Youth Services, founded in 1974, provides through human services agencies assistance to runaway and homeless youth, alternatives for at-risk youths and their families. This organization also serves as a clearinghouse for information and programs for the general public.

Titles:
Access to Health Care for Runaway and Homeless Youth: Summary Report. 1991
Being an Effective Youth Advocate: A National Network Guide. 1989
Gender: A Guide to Addressing Gender and Relationship Issues with Young People. 1992
Network News. Quarterly
Policy Reporter. 8/year
Safe Choices Guide: AIDS and HIV Policies and Prevention Programs for High-Risk Youth. 1990

Subject Headings:
Runaway teenagers
Social work with youth
Youth

[116]
NATIONAL RURAL HEALTH ASSOCIATION
National Headquarters
1320 19th Street NW, Suite 350
Washington, DC 20036-1610
(202) 232-6200
National Service Center
One West Armour Boulevard, Suite 301
Kansas City, MO 64111
(816) 756-3140
(816) 756-3144 Fax

History and Goals: Established in 1978 as the National Rural Primary Care Association. Major bylaw changes and restructuring occurred in 1984 and the organization name was changed to the National Rural Health Care Association. In 1986, the organization merged with the American Small and Rural Hospital Association. Later that year, the National Rural Health Care Association and the American Rural Health Association voted to merge. The new association began its operation in 1987, under the new name, the National Rural Health Association. The Association strives to improve the health of rural Americans and to provide leadership on rural issues through advocacy, communications, education, and research. The Association works to create a better understanding of health and health care problems unique to rural areas. They also communicate the health care views of rural Americans and works to develop positive solutions. Membership includes administrators, educators, students, researchers, government workers, physicians and other private practice health professionals, hospitals, community and migrant health centers, and government and educational institutions.

Titles:
Health and Aging in Rural America. 1994
Health Care in Frontier America: A Time for Change. 1994
Journal of Rural Health. Quarterly
Rural Clinician Quarterly. Quarterly
Rural Health Care: The Newsletter of the National Rural Health Association. Bimonthly
Rural Health FYI. Bimonthly
Rural Health Resources Directory. 1994

A Shared Vision: Building Bridges for Rural Health Access. 1994
Working Together for Change: How to Establish a State Rural Health Association. 1993

Subject Headings:
Medical care
Rural health

[117]
NATIONAL RURAL HOUSING COALITION
601 Pennsylvania Avenue, NW, Suite 850
Washington, DC 20004
(202) 393-5229
(202) 393-3034 Fax

History and Goals: The NRHC was formed in 1969 by a concerned group of rural and community activists, public officials, and nonprofit developers to fight for better housing and community facilities for low income and rural people. This organization lobbies Congress directly and through a network of rural housing advocates to address the needs of rural areas. The Coalition regularly sponsors conferences and are entirely supported by donations and subscriptions. The chief goal of the NHRC is to serve the rural poor.

Titles:
FmHa Notes. Serial
Legislative Update. Biweekly

Subject Headings:
Housing
Poor

[118]
NORTH AMERICAN ASSOCIATION OF CHRISTIANS IN SOCIAL WORK
Box 7090
St. David's, PA 19087-7090
(610) 687-5777
(610) 687-5777 Fax

History and Goals: The NACSW developed out of a series of annual conferences which began in 1950 and was incorporated in 1954. It exists as an interdenominational and international organization of people committed to integrating the Christian faith and social work practice. The Association's main objectives are to provide Christian social workers with opportunities for education, personal growth, and fellowship; to promote a Christian world view through social work; and to encourage awareness of contemporary human need which the profession of social work can address. The NACSW holds an annual conference and has approximately 1,000 members.

Titles:
Catalyst. Bimonthly
A Christian Response to Domestic Violence: A Reconciliation Model for Social Workers. 1985
Church Social Work: Helping the Whole Person in the Context of the Church. 1992
Encounters With Children: Stories That Help Us Understand and Help Them. 1991
Integrating Faith and Practice: A History of the North American Association of Christians in Social Work. 1994
The Poor You Have With You Always: Concepts of Aid to the Poor in the Western World from Biblical Times to the Present. 1989

Social Work and Christianity. Semiannual
So You Want To Be A Social Worker: A Primer for the Christian Student. 1985
Spirit-Led Helping: A Model for Evangelical Social Work Counseling. 1987

Subject Headings:
Church work with children
Social service
Social work with children

[119]
NORTH AMERICAN COUNCIL ON ADOPTABLE CHILDREN
970 Raymond Avenue, Suite 106
St. Paul, MN 55114-1149
(612) 644-3036
(612) 644-9848 Fax

History and Goals: NACAC is a nonprofit, broad based coalition of agencies, volunteer adoptive parent support and citizen advocacy groups working together to meet the needs of children waiting to be adopted in the United States and Canada. This organization sponsors a national conference on adoption issues; provides consultation and public education services; disseminates adoption research and publications; and works as an advocate on adoption issues. The Council is funded through membership dues and publication sales.

Titles:
Adoptalk Newsletter. Quarterly
The Adoption Assistance and Child Welfare Act of 1980: The First Ten Years. 1990
Barriers to Same Race Placement. 1991
Challenges to Child Welfare: Countering the Call for a Return to Orphanages. 1990
Family Preservation, the Second Time Around: A Curriculum for Adoptive Families. 1992
User's Guide to P.L. 96–272: A Summarization and Codification of Administrative Issuances. 1992

Subject Headings:
Adoption
Child welfare

[120]
OLDER WOMEN'S LEAGUE
666 Eleventh Street, NW, Suite 700
Washington, DC 20001
(800) 825-3695
(202) 783-6686
(202) 638-2356 Fax

History and Goals: This national organization was founded in 1980 by Tish Sommers and Laurie Shields to fight for the rights of mid-life and older women. OWL recognizes that aging impacts women differently than men and addresses the formidable issues brought on my aging. The main goals of OWL are to achieve social and economic equity for aging women and to provide support to its 20,000 members. OWL has developed a national agenda to fight for universal health care, more equitable Social Security benefits, improved employer-sponsored pension programs, and better housing options. This tax-exempt organization holds regular conventions and has many types of publications for sale.

Titles:

Critical Condition: Mid-life and Older Women in American's Health Care System. 1992

Ending Violence Against Midlife and Older Women: A Mother's Day Call to Action. 1994

The Field Advocate. Monthly

First Line of Defense Handbook. 1994

The Future of Housing: Alone and Female in the 21st Century. 1993

Heading for Hardship: Retirement Income for American Women in the Next Century. 1990

In Search of a Solution: The American Health Care Crisis. 1991

Money and the Mature Woman. 1993

OWL Observer. Bimonthly

Path to Poverty: An Analysis of Women's Retirement Income. 1995

Paying for Prejudice: Mid-life and Older Women in America's Labor Force. 1992

Room for Improvement: The Lack of Affordable, Adaptable and Accessible Housing for Midlife and Older Women. 1993

Sexually Transmitted Disease Survey: The Dangers of Denial. 1994

Subject Headings:

Aging

Women

[121]
PAN AMERICAN HEALTH ORGANIZATION

525 23rd Street, NW
Washington, DC 20037
(202) 861-3200
(202) 223-5971 Fax
Internet Site: http://www.paho.org/

History and Goals: This Organization was founded in 1902 to unite nations in the Western Hemisphere to improve all health care in the Americas. The Organization sponsors programs and provides consulting services. Many of the publications are in English as well as Spanish.

Titles:

Bulletin of PAHO. Quarterly

The Crisis of Public Health: Reflections for the Debate. 1992

Disaster Preparedness in the Americas. Quarterly

EPI Newsletter. Bimonthly

Epidemiological Bulletin. Bimonthly

Ethics and Law in the Study of AIDS. 1992

Gender, Women, and Health. 1993

Health Care for the Poor in Latin America and the Caribbean. 1992

Health Conditions in the Americas. Quadrennial

Health Services Research: An Anthology. 1992

Health Statistics from the Americas, 1992 Edition. 1993

Implementation of the Global Strategy for Health for All by the Year 2000. 1993

Subject Headings:

Health

Medical care

[122]
PLANNED PARENTHOOD FEDERATION OF AMERICA
810 Seventh Avenue
New York, NY 10019-5882
(212) 541-7800
(800) 669-0156 Publications
(212) 669-0156 Fax
Internet Site: http://www.iti.com/iti/kzpg/pp.html

History and Goals: Planned Parenthood, founded in 1916 by Margaret Sanger, is one of the largest voluntary reproductive health care organizations in the United States dedicated to the fundamental right that every individual has a right to choose when and whether to have children. The activities of Planned Parenthood include providing for comprehensive reproductive and complementary health care services to all, advocating public policies which guarantee reproductive rights and access to services, developing educational programs on human sexuality, and promoting research and advancement of technology in reproductive health care. The Federation also works to provide international family planning services in over 100 countries. Publications include books, pamphlets, and videotapes.

Titles:
10 Minutes to Better Board Meetings. 1994
AIDS and HIV: Questions and Answers. 1993
Facts About Birth Control. 1993
A Family Planning Library Manual. 5th rev. ed. 1993
Planned Parenthood Women's Health Letter. Bimonthly
Redirecting Boards: A New Vision of Governance for Planned Parenthood. 1993
A Tradition of Choice: Planned Parenthood. 1991

Subject Headings:
Birth control

[123]
THE POPULATION COUNCIL
1 Dag Hammerskjold Plaza
New York, NY 10017-2220
(212) 339-0514
(212) 755-6052 Fax
Internet Site: http://www.popcouncil.org/

History and Goals: This international, nonprofit organization was established in 1952 with the goal of finding solutions to population problems in developing countries. Their work focuses on family planning and fertility, reproductive health and child survival, women's roles and status, the introduction of contraceptives, population policy, and the dissemination of information and publications.

Titles:
Families at the Dawn of a New Century: Changing Perspectives on the Roles of Mothers, Fathers, and Children. 1994
Family and Gender Issues for Population Policy. 1993
Family Planning and Population: A Compendium of International Statistics. 1993
Findings From Two Decades of Family Planning Research. 1993

Household Structure and Poverty: What Are the Connections. 1995
The New Politics of Population: Conflict and Consensus in Family Planning. 1994
Population and Development Review. Quarterly
Population Briefs: Reports on Population Council Research. Quarterly
Resources, Environment, and Population: Present Knowledge, Future Options. 1991
Studies in Family Planning. Bimonthly

Subject Headings:
Birth control

[124]
POPULATION REFERENCE BUREAU
1875 Connecticut Avenue NW, Suite 520
Washington, DC 20009-5728
(202) 483-1100
(202) 328-9337 Fax
Internet Site: http://www.prb.org/prb/

History and Goals: The Population Reference Bureau was established in 1929 and is a private, nonprofit organization that gathers, interprets and disseminates information about population. The PRB seeks to increase understanding of population trends and their public policy implications.

Titles:
Americans on the Move. 1993
The Baby Boom—Entering Midlife. 1991
A Demographic Portrait of South and Southeast Asia: A Chartbook. 1994
The Future of the World Population. 1994
Leaving and Returning Home in 20th Century America. 1994
New Realities of the American Family. 1992
Paths to Demographic Change in the Near East and North Africa: A Chartbook. 1994
Population Bulletin. Quarterly
Population Today. Monthly
Population Trends and Public Policy. Serial
Where's Papa? Fathers' Role in Child Care. 1993

Subject Headings:
Birth control
Family policy
Population

[125]
POVERTY AND RACE RESEARCH ACTION COUNCIL
1711 Connecticut Avenue, NW, Suite 207
Washington, DC 20009
(202) 387-9887
(202) 387-0764 Fax

History and Goals: PRACC is a new national organization that works to link social science research to advocacy work in order to successfully address race and poverty issues. This grant-giving organization funds research tied to local, state and national advocacy strategies; coordinates strategy in race and poverty areas by enhancing communication between advocates and researchers; and distributes materials and holds conferences focusing on race and poverty issues. PRACC has established a network of over 5,000 researchers and advocates working together on these issues.

Titles:

Poverty and Race. Bimonthly
PRAAC Network Directory. 1994

Subject Headings:

Poverty
Race relations

[126]
RESEARCH AND TRAINING CENTER ON FAMILY SUPPORT AND CHILDREN'S MENTAL HEALTH

Regional Research Institute for Human Services
Portland State University
P.O. Box 751
Portland, OR 97207-0751
(503) 725-4040
(503) 725-4180 Fax
(800) 628-1696 National Clearinghouse

History and Goals: The Center was created in 1984 and is funded through government grants. The purpose of the Center is to improve services for families whose children have serious mental, emotional or behavioral disorders. Staff members have established a clearinghouse to provide resource materials to families and mental health professionals.

Titles:

Family Research and Demonstration Symposium Report. 1993
Focal Point. Triennial
Issues in Culturally Competent Service Delivery: An Annotated Bibliography. 1990
National Directory of Organizations Serving Parents of Children and Youth with Emotional and Behavioral Disorders. 3rd ed. 1993
Therapeutic Case Advocacy Workers' Handbook. 1990

Subject Headings:

Mentally ill children
Social work with minorities
Socially handicapped children

[127]
THE ROPER CENTER FOR PUBLIC OPINION

University of Connecticut
Montieth Building Room 421
341 Mansfield Road
Storrs, CT 06269
(860) 486-4440
(860) 486-6308 Fax

History and Goals: The Roper Center, a nonprofit, nonpartisan public opinion data archive, was founded shortly after World War II by Elmo Roper. Roper, along with George Gallup, was responsible for the development of the Center. They established survey organizations which continue to contribute data to the library even to the present day. The Roper Center maintains a world-renowned collection of domestic and international public opinion information for the purpose of improving the practice of survey research and for promoting the responsible use of public opinion data in facing issues worldwide. The Center is accessible to academic and policy researchers.

Titles:
America at the Polls, 1994. 1995
General Social Surveys, 1972–1994. 1994
The Public Perspective. Bimonthly

Subject Headings:
Elections
Population
Public opinion

[128]
SAGE: SENIOR ACTION IN A GAY ENVIRONMENT
305 7th Avenue, 16th Fl.
New York, NY 10001
(212) 741-2247
(212) 366-1947 Fax

History and Goals:. Founded in 1978 in New York City, SAGE provides services to the gay and lesbian elderly. Counseling, case management and advocacy are activities/services provided by trained volunteers including lawyers, doctors, social workers, gerontologists, and psychologists. Programs include a gay and lesbian senior center, AIDS and the Elderly Program and Clinic Treadmill Program. SAGE focuses on AIDS and mental health issues; education and training in gay and lesbian aging issues.

Titles:
Newsletter. Monthly

Subject Headings:
Aged
Gays
Lesbians

[129]
SAVE THE CHILDREN FEDERATION
54 Wilton Road
Westport, CT 06880
(203) 221-4000
(800) 243-5074
(203) 454-3914 Fax
Internet Site: http:www.charity.com/save.html

History and Goals: Save the Children is an international relief and community development organization founded in 1932. The Federation works with families and countries throughout the world. Community-based self-help programs are designed by the Federation to improve living conditions and increase opportunities for children and families to live healthy, productive lives.

Titles:
Community Reports. Semiannual
HIV/AIDS. 1992
Impact Magazine. Quarterly
Rural Family Friends Replication Manual. 1992
Save the Children Reports. Periodic

Subject Headings:
Child health services
Children
Hunger

[130]
SEX INFORMATION AND EDUCATION COUNCIL OF THE U.S. (SIECUS)
130 West 42nd St.
Suite 350
New York, NY 10036
(212) 819-9770
(212) 819-9776 Fax

History and Goals: Founded in 1964, SIECUS includes educators, social workers, physicians, clergy, youth organizations, parents' groups, and others concerned about human sexuality education and sexual health care. Goals are to support and examine scientific research on human sexuality; disseminate data and provide education, training and leadership programs in the field of human sexuality, and to identify, develop, and promote social policies that foster positive attitudes, values, and practices related to human sexuality. The Council conducts seminars and internship programs, offers technical assistance, operates an information service and a 4,500 volume library.

Titles:
SIECUS' Community Action Kit: An Information Pack To Support Comprehensive Sexuality Education. 1993
SIECUS Developments. Semiannual
SIECUS Newsletter. Quarterly
SIECUS Report. Bimonthly

Subject Headings:
Sex role

[131]
STONE CENTER
Wellesley College
106 Central Street
Wellesley, MA 02181-8268
(617) 235-0320 ext. 2838

History and Goals: The Stone Center was created by an endowment in 1981 with the charge of preventing mental illness through education, research, community outreach, and counseling programs. The Center sponsors free public lectures, conducts workshops, provides training seminars, holds conferences, disseminates a newsletter, and publishes and sells conference reports, audio tapes, videotapes, and working papers.

Titles:
Borderline Personality Disorder and Childhood Abuse. 1991
Surviving Incest: One Woman's Struggle for Connection. 1991
Women, Addiction and Codependency. 1991
The Woman-Man Relationship: Impasses and Possibilities. 1992

Subject Headings:
Mental health

[132]
STUDY CIRCLES RESOURCES CENTER
P.O. Box 203
Pomfret, CT 06258
(203) 928-2616
(203) 928-3713 Fax

History and Goals: Founded in 1990 and sponsored by Topsfield Foundation, Inc., Study Circles Resources Center promotes the discussion of significant social and political issues. These issues are explored through the use of study circles, a method whereby a group of 5-20 people gather together to share their viewpoints. Additionally, the Center publishes discussions, programs and how-to materials on topics such as racism, the environment, health and welfare reform, and provides a clearinghouse list of organizations who have developed study circle materials.

Titles:
Can't We All Just Get Along? A Manual for Discussion Programs on Racism and Race Relations. 1992
The Death Penalty in the United States. 1993
Focus on Study Circles. Quarterly
Immigrants, Your Community and U.S. Policy. 1993
In Harm's Way: When Should We Risk American Lives in World Conflicts? 1994
Welfare Reform: What Should We Do for Our Nation's Poor? 1992

Subject Headings:
Social problems

[133]
UNITED STATES COMMITTEE FOR REFUGEES
1717 Massachusetts Avenue, NW, Suite 701
Washington, DC 20036
(202) 347-3507
(202) 347-3418 Fax

History and Goals: Founded in 1958, the United States Committee for Refugees, through its regional affiliates, helps immigrants and refugees adapt to American life. The Committee also assists immigrants through practical means, such as assistance with language learning and immigration laws, and also by working to improve immigration and naturalization laws.

Titles:
Issue Papers. Quarterly
Refugee Reports. Monthly
World Refugee Survey. Annual

Subject Headings:
Ethnic relations
Refugees
Social work with immigrants

[134]
UNITED STATES CONFERENCE OF MAYORS
1620 Eye Street NW
Washington, DC 20006
(202) 293-7330
(202) 293-2352 Fax

History and Goals: This nonpartisan organization was established in 1932 and represents cities with populations of 30,000 or more people. The Conference of Mayors works to improve city government and aids in the development of national urban policy. The Conference also works to help mayors to gain leadership and management experience. The Mayors adopt urban policy positions, lobby Congress, and hold an annual conference.

Titles:
Access to Health Care for Minorities: Profiles of 3 Local Health Departments. 1992
Best Practices of City Governments. 1995
Education and Service Coordination for Asymptomatic HIV-Infected Women and Injection Drug Users: A Review of Community Based HIV Prevention Programs Funded by the United States Conference of Mayors. 1993
HIV Prevention Community Planning Profiles: Assessing Year One. 1995
Local AIDS Services: The National Directory. 1994
Mentally Ill and Homeless: A 22-City Survey. 1991
1992 Allied Membership Directory. 1992
A Status Report on Hunger and Homelessness in America's Cities, 1992: A 29-City Survey. 1992

Subject Headings:
Community health services
Homelessness
Urban policy

[135]
URBAN INSTITUTE
UPA Order Department
4720 Boston Way, Suite A
Lanham, MD 20706
(301) 459-3366
(800) 462-6420 (Customer service)
(301) 459-2118 Fax
Internet Site: http://www.urban.org/

History and Goals: Urban Institute is a nonprofit policy research and educational organization established in 1968. Its staff investigates the social and economic problems confronting the national and government policies and programs designed to alleviate such problems. The Institute's two goals are to help shape thinking about societal problems and efforts to solve them, and to improve government decisions and performance by providing better information and analytic tools.

Titles:

America's Homeless: Numbers, Characteristics, and Programs that Serve Them. 1989

Child Poverty and Public Policy. 1993

Effects of Immigration on Wages and Joblessness: Evidence from Thirty Demographic Groups. 1995

Guide to the Federal Budget. Annual

Immigration and Ethnicity: The Integration of America's Newest Arrivals. 1994

Medicaid Since 1980: Costs, Coverage, and the Shifting Alliance Between the Federal Government and the States. 1994

National Child Care Survey, 1990. 1991

Nurturing Young Black Males: Challenges to Agencies, Programs, and Social Policy. 1994

Retooling Social Security for the 21st Century: Right and Wrong Approaches to Reform. 1994

Status and Prospects of the Nonprofit Housing Sector. 1995

Subject Headings:

Child welfare

Social security

Urban policy

[136]
WILLIAM MONROE TROTTER INSTITUTE

University of Massachusetts–Boston

Harbor Campus

100 Morrissey Boulevard

Wheatley Building, 4th Floor, Room 98

Boston, MA 02125-3393

(617) 287-5880

History and Goals: This Institute was founded in 1984 with the charge of addressing the issues of the Black community in Massachusetts through public service and research. The Institute regularly sponsors public forums to present research findings and to involve the Black community in public policy discussions. The Institute also provides technical assistance to community groups and organizations.

Titles:

African Americans in the Military. 1993

Assessment of the Status of African Americans. 1990

Health and Medical Care of African Americans. 1992

A Historical Overview of Poverty Among Blacks in Boston 1850–1990. 1994

Missing Links in the Study of Puerto Rican Poverty in the United States. 1995

The Role of the Urban League Movement in Overcoming Inner-City Poverty: Challenges for the 21st Century. 1995

Trotter Review. Triennial

Subject Headings:

Afro Americans

Puerto Ricans

[137]
W.E. UPJOHN INSTITUTE FOR EMPLOYMENT RESEARCH
300 South Westnedge Avenue
Kalamazoo, MI 49007-4686
(616) 343-4330 (Publications)
(616) 343-7310 Fax

History and Goals: The W.E. Upjohn Institute was established in 1945 as a nonprofit research organization with the mission of finding solutions to employment-related problems at local, state, and national levels. The Institute provides grants and conducts and supports policy-oriented research in many areas. The Institute's main objectives are to combine scholarship and experimentation with issues of public and private employment and unemployment policy, and to apply new knowledge to find solutions to employment and unemployment problems.

Titles:

Classrooms in the Workplace: Workplace Literacy Programs in Small- and Medium-Sized Firms.
   1993

The Costs of Worker's Dislocation. 1993

The Economics of Comparable Worth. 1990

Federal Policy Towards State and Local Economic Development in the 1990's. 1993

Human Capital and Economic Development. 1994

Improving Access to Health Care: What Can the States Do? 1992

Measuring Employment and Training Program Impacts with Data on Program Applicants. 1995

Pathways to Change: Strategic Choices in Labor Negotiations. 1995

Pension Incentives and Job Mobility. 1994

Private Pension Policies in Industrialized Countries: A Comparative Analysis. 1994

Program Applicants as a Comparison Group in Evaluating Training Programs: Theory and a Test.
   1995

Unemployment Insurance in the United States: The First Half Century. 1993

Subject Headings:
Employment
Social policy

TITLE INDEX

F

I

J

M

N

O

P

R

S

SUBJECT INDEX

STATE INDEX